THE ESSENTIAL GUIDE TO TEACHING KEYBOARDING IN 45 MINUTES A WEEK

A K-8 Curriculum

by The Structured Learning IT Team and Ask a Tech Teacher

First Edition 2012
Part of the Structured Learning Technology for the Classroom series
Visit the companion website at http://askatechteacher.com for more resources to teach technology to Kindergarten-Eighth Grade

To receive free weekly digital technology tips and/or websites, email admin@structuredlearning.net with the message "Subscribe to Weekly Tips" or "Subscribe to Weekly Websites"

ISBN 978-0-9845881-6-9

Printed in the United States of America

Table of Contents

Introduction

You may think it impossible to find a keyboarding curriculum that creates accomplished typists from the skimpy forty-five minutes a week you can devote to keyboarding. You teach what you can, but it always seems to be the same lessons—hands on home row, good posture, eyes on copy. You wonder if it's making a difference.

Every year, you promise it will go better and then it doesn't. You're thinking of giving up. You have lots of friends who hunt-and-peck as adults and are doing fine. Does it even matter if students learn to touch type?

Yes, it matters, and there is a way to teach them—that works. It requires a plan, faithfully executed, with your eye relentlessly on the goal, but if you commit to that, it works. K-8 students have the finger dexterity—they play piano and the like quite well—to type, just not the knowledge. Research also tells us that children who learn to keyboard improve academically (Wood and Freeman 1931; Erickson 1959). It makes sense that it should be one of school's essential skills.

In *The Essential Guide to Teaching Keyboarding in 45 Minutes a Week: a K-8 Curriculum*, one grade at a time, I'll share a keyboard curriculum for K-8 that I've seen work on thousands of students. You'll find directions on what to do, how and when, using mostly free resources. The biggest cost is the price of this short textbook. Consider this the keyboarding version of Strunk and White's Elements of Style—everything you need in 110 (give or take) pages.

Objectives

The overarching objective of keyboarding is to **facilitate communication of ideas**. That means first, students must type fast enough to exceed the speed of their handwriting, and second, they must keep up with their thoughts. Done as described in this book, the former will occur around fourth grade and the latter around seventh or eighth.

How to Use This Book

For each grade, the lesson organization is clear, with sections to address what you need to know to teach that grade level to keyboard.

Here's a sample:

At the **beginning** of each grade-level section:

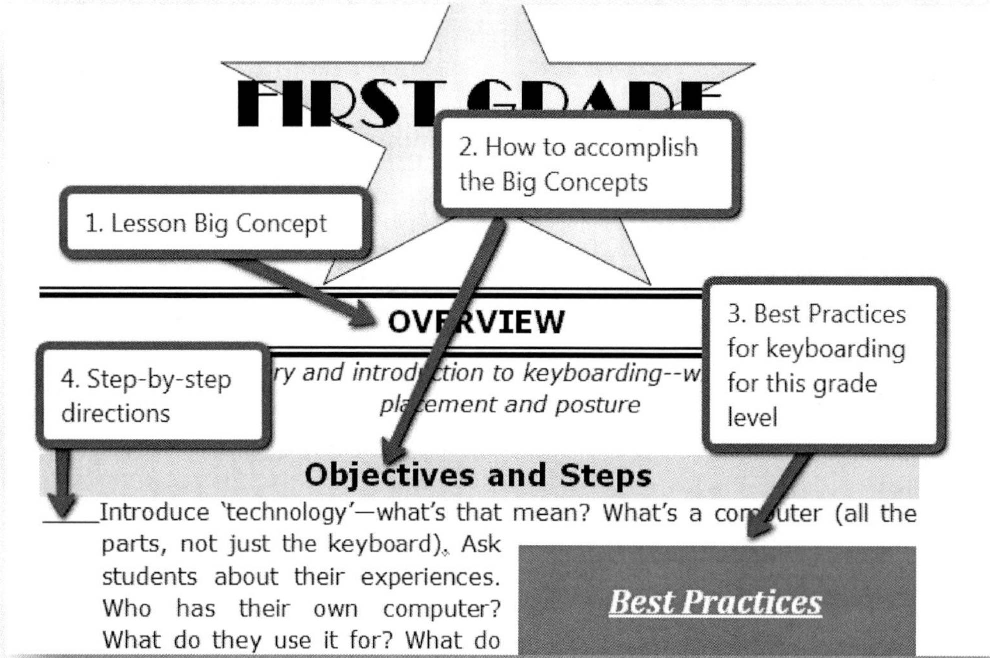

At the **end** of each grade-level section:

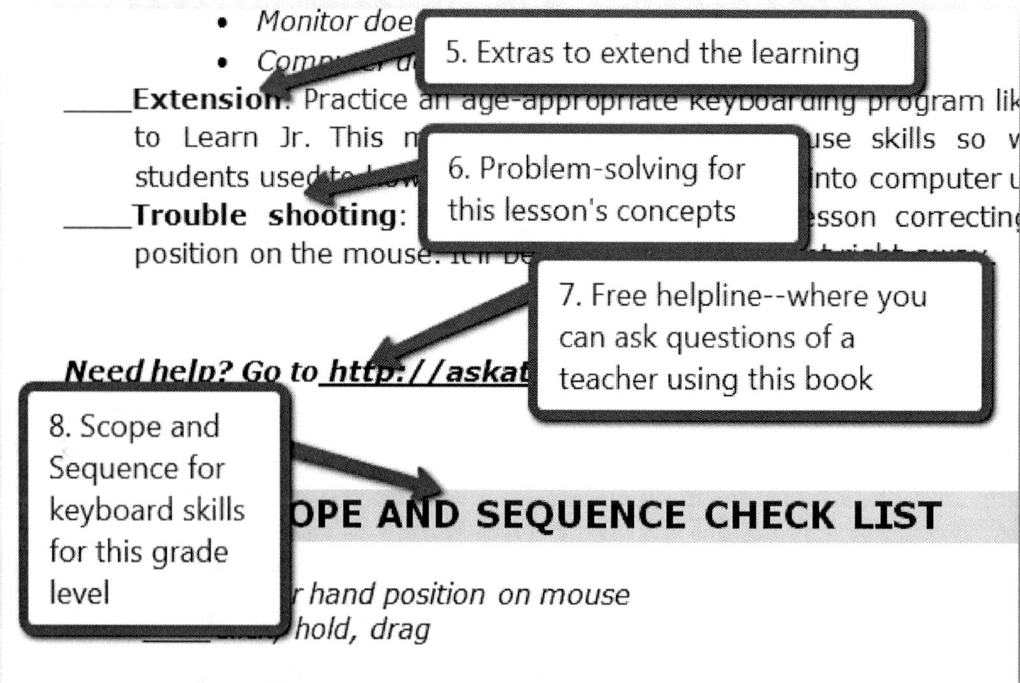

1. ***Overview***—*overarching skills to be accomplished at this grade level.*
2. ***Objectives and Steps***—*practical strategies for achieving the lesson's essential goals with step-by-step guidelines to show evidence of accomplishment*
3. ***Best Practices***—*Essential items that scaffold comprehension of the big concepts*
4. ***Step-by-step—****check off each objective as it is accomplished*
5. ***Extension***—*Ideas to extend learning, vertically plan, and/or encourage student risk-taking (located at end of section)*
6. ***Trouble-shooting***—*how to problem-solve possible difficulties (located at end of section)*
7. ***Need Help***—*a website that provides free help on this lesson from teachers who use the curriculum (located at end of section)*
8. ***Scope and Sequence***—*checklist of skills to be accomplished at this grade-level. Be sure to complete all of them before moving onto the next grade level. The curriculum's success depends upon this simple commitment (after Objectives and Steps section)*

You'll find a lot of links in this book. They are **extras in the digital ebook**—as are full color images and being able to search with Ctrl+F. To put them in the print version would take oh-so-much-space and ultimately be oh-so-confusing. If you would like a PDF of the book so links are available, contact the publisher (http://structuredlearning.net) to get a discounted PDF with your Proof of Purchase. If there are just one or two links you're curious about, visit the helpline (that's Ask a Tech Teacher noted at the end of each grade-level section) and leave a request as a comment on the most current article. Be sure to include the book name and page number. I'll answer within 24 hours.

As a bonus, we've included nine articles on pedagogic topics like *What About Those Lefties, Summer Keyboarding Class–Here are the Details,* and *Is Keyboarding Dead?*

Research

If you're like many teachers I've talked to, you are asking yourself (or parents in your school are asking) the following questions before committing the time necessary for a comprehensive keyboarding program:

1. *Can elementary school children learn to keyboard?*
2. *What is the best age to begin keyboarding?*
3. *How important is it that the teacher be knowledgeable about typing?*
4. *Is it still important that students learn keyboarding?*

Here are the quick answers:

1. *Yes—emphatically*
2. *As soon as students use a computer*
3. *Extremely*
4. *Of course!*

Don't take my word for it. Read the research.

Can K-8 Children Learn to Keyboard?

An overview of research says **yes**, elementary- and middle school-age students are cognitively, emotionally, and physically capable of learning keyboarding skills. Just as with piano and violin (and any number of sports), their fine motor skills, mental processes, and physiologic development are mature enough for the demands of typing.

But let's dig deeper.

Developmentally, some researchers maintain keyboarding is too abstract for immature brains and too demanding of undeveloped fine motor skills to learn at a young age.

Let's look at that claim. In order for the skill of keyboarding to be mastered, one must be able to let fingers flow freely (Waner, Behymer, & McCrary, 1992), a concept backed by Bloom's idea of automaticity and discussed by Wronkovich (1998), who defines it as a "system of automatic habits corresponding to the system of tasks".

I agree—keyboarding requires this "system of automatic habits". Is that a reasonable expectation of the K-8 child?

Yes and no. To ask a kindergartner (or a first/second grader) to concentrate on what each finger is doing is unreasonable and not age-appropriate. However, it is just as unreasonable to NOT expect a sixth-eighth grader to be able to accomplish these.

The key is to introduce skills that are **age-appropriate**.

Best Age to Teach Keyboarding

Most researchers agree effective keyboarding isn't instinctual and should be begun **before bad habits are created**. But when does that happen? Is elementary school too early—or too late?

> *Children often develop their own inefficient hunt-and-peck systems that take longer, waste limited computer time, and develop habits that are difficult to change.*
> *--Type to Learn 1986*

Research varies on this topic. Bartholome (1996) found that third grade is appropriate for touch keyboarding, but first and second graders can learn this skill as well if given adequate instruction. This conclusion was reinforced by Feutz (2001).

On the opposite side is Erthal (2002) who found that third graders do not possess the manual dexterity required for keyboarding, and Hopkins (1998) who considered fourth grade an appropriate age for the commencement of formal keyboarding.

We are left with a mushy consensus among researchers that third-fifth grade is the appropriate time to begin keyboarding skills.

But fifth grade may be too late. Young children are in front of keyboards earlier than ever. In the absence of training, they will still learn, likely wrong. Therefore, logic dictates that **when students start to use computers to type, they should be taught correct keyboarding practices**. From my experience, that's third grade with this caveat: Teach pre-keyboard skills kindergarten-second grade before beginning the focus on traditional skills of posture-speed-accuracy.

Importance of Teacher Knowledge

Sormunen's 1991 study found that classroom instructors were teaching keyboarding, but only 12% had any formal preparation in how to do that.

> *...only a small proportion of classroom teachers have any formal preparation for teaching keyboarding.*
> *Sormunen, 1991*

Condon's study (1989) found that educational administrators felt elementary teachers should be provided with sufficient training to teach keyboarding. McLean (1994) suggested that instruction can be supplied by teachers who have taken a keyboarding methods course, or a business education teacher who has had elementary learning methods, or a combination of both.

Consensus of most studies indicates that a "knowledgeable" teacher is critical to help students develop appropriate techniques, as well as provide motivation and reinforcement (Nieman, 1996; Erthal, 1998).

Importance of Learning Keyboarding

Many studies document the value of children learning proper typing technique (McKay, 1998; Owston, 1997; Bartholome, 1996; Bieman, 1996; Hoot, 1986). Rogers (2003) lists the following eight benefits:

> *Student writing develops faster through word processing because it facilitates the review and revision learning process.*
> *Zeitz, 2008*
> *http://im.ly/ed3bd/*

1. *Improvement in language arts—reading, spelling, and writing*
2. *Improvement in efficiency using computers as writing, editing, and computing tools, thereby maximizing classroom time*
3. *Improvement in attitude toward writing—less frustration in looking for keys rather that entering information*

4. *Improvement in proper keyboarding techniques and use of the computer, thereby eliminating the formation of bad keyboarding habits for later word processing and computer applications*
5. *Improvement in motivating students toward doing schoolwork*
6. *Improvement in creative thought*
7. *Improvement in integrating keyboarding with all subject areas*
8. *Improvement in preparing all students for a technological society*

How to Teach Keyboarding in K-8

Two criteria are mentioned over and over in keyboarding research:

1. *Keyboarding instruction is most effective when spread out over several years and designed to build on the student's prior knowledge. (Robinson 1992)*
2. *Once skills are taught, it is important to use them, reinforce them and refine them (Adams, 1984; Wronkovich, 1998).*

I agree and have made these cornerstones to my curriculum for fifteen years. Here's an overview of my keyboarding focus for grades K-8:

K-1	*Introduce mouse skills and keyboarding while focusing on key placement and posture*
2nd	*Introduce keyboarding while focusing on key placement, posture, and two-hand position*
3rd	*Reinforce basics of key position, posture and hand position while beginning accuracy and technique*
4-5	*Reinforce key position, posture and hand position. Continue work on accuracy and technique. Begin focus on speed with age-appropriate speed-and-accuracy goals*
6-8	*Work on all essential elements of keyboarding—technique, speed, and accuracy—with grade level goal of 35-45 wpm*

Class lessons must include lots of variety so no one gets bored with the mundanity of typing. Here's a rundown of the pieces I include (more detail later on how to incorporate them at each grade level):

- *Classroom keyboarding software*

- *Online keyboarding websites*
- *Age-appropriate use of hand covers (grades 2-8)*
- *Quarterly speed/accuracy quizzes (grades 3-8)*
- *Quarterly blank keyboarding quizzes (grades 3-8)*
- *Monthly homework (grades 3-8)*
- *Wall chart on those who meet/exceed grade level expectations*
- *Wall chart tracking student progress throughout the year*
- *Wall chart showing which students type faster than they can handwrite*
- *Wall charts on important keys, body position*
- *Grading based on student improvement, not conformity to class norms*

Body Position

Seat
Position chair facing keyboard about one hand's-width from the table with keyboard one inch off edge of table.

Head and eyes
Place monitor so eyes look straight ahead with neck straight, not bent too far forward or back.

Body and Hands
Sit straight with elbows tucked against sides. Keep body natural, easy and relaxed with feet on the floor slightly apart. Keep fingers curved over keys, resting on home row.

Questions You May Have

In my class, keyboarding is the most-asked topic with parents. On my blog (Ask a Tech Teacher), keyboarding posts are read thrice as often as any other topic. Based on research (see above) and my fifteen years experience teaching thousands of students, here are answers to some of the critical questions:

Why learn keyboarding?
If you've ever seen a third grader struggle to type a web address into the computer or type a book report when they don't know where the keys are, you know they should have started keyboarding earlier.

That's the first reason. There are more:

- *to communicate ideas*
- *to find out more about what interests them*
- *to offset a learning disability that interferes with writing–i.e., dysgraphia*

When should children learn keyboarding?
Today's children interact with keyboards from an early age and as a result are in danger of learning bad habits if they aren't taught early rather than late. In short, students should learn to keyboard:

- *when teachers expect projects that require keyboarding*
- *when a child's interests dictate a demand for typing*
- *when students are expected to use classroom computers*
- *by fourth grade: A trained fourth grader can write and type at the same speed*

What are some of keyboarding's developmental considerations?
In a macro sense, correct keyboarding takes into account cognitive maturity, fine motor skills and age-appropriateness of skills taught.

These three factors are constantly considered and adapted for in these lessons.

How do I (Ask a Tech Teacher) teach keyboarding?
I teach pre-keyboarding skills like posture, hand position, mouse skills, key placement, before starting technique. I make all lessons age-appropriate:

- *Kindergarten is about mouse skills, getting hands on the keyboard and learning good posture*
- *First grade is about getting hands on the correct side of the keyboard and forming good habits*
- *Second grade is about understanding that fingers type different keys—and good posture*
- *Third grade starts touch typing–use the right finger for the right key, make good posture a habit*

- *Fourth grade is about memorizing key placement, keeping eyes on the screen, and posture*
- *Fifth-eighth grade is about speed and accuracy*

I teach finger exercises to remind students they have eight fingers and a thumb (they don't use the left thumb). These make keyboarding fun.

I teach key placement first, using programs like Big Brown Bear Typing for kindergarten-first grade and a blank keyboard exercise for olders

I teach touch typing starting no sooner than third grade. I get serious about key memorization in fourth grade.

I teach shortkeys at all grade levels. Students feel good when they can zip out a shortkey instead of struggling with an awkward combination of keys.

I keep it fun

What about keyboard homework?
You'll see it in grades three-five.

Why is keyboarding a 'hot topic' with parents?

- Kids want to use the computer; parents want them outside playing
- Teachers are asking for computer projects
- The child sees something on the computer–Starfall.com or Santa traveling across the holiday sky–and wants to go there

Will keyboarding replace cursive writing?

- Not until input devices are more available–but why not?

What are good online sites to practice keyboarding?
Start with these twenty:

1. Big Brown Bear typing–great for grades kindergarten, first
2. Typing Web–a log-in allows you to track progress
3. Test Your Typing--see if you're improving
4. Keyboard challenge—adapted to grade level
5. Keyboard practice—quick start

6. Keyboarding Fingerjig—6 minute test of ability
7. Keyboarding for Kids
8. Keyboarding practice
9. Keyboarding—alphabet rain game
10. Keyboarding—barracuda game
11. Keyboarding—bubbles game
12. Dance Mat Typing — very popular with grades 3-5; lots of fun
13. Keyboarding—full online course
14. Keyboarding—games
15. Keyboarding—lessons and speed quiz
16. Keyboarding—lessons
17. Keyboarding—more lessons
18. Keyboarding—must sign up, but free
19. Keyboarding—quick start
20. Keyboarding—speed quiz

How do I fix a broken keyboard?

You sit down to type that long project with the imminent deadline, and nothing happens. The cursor blinks... and blinks... and blinks... but goes nowhere. What do you do?

Before you go buy a new keyboard, try these:

- *Is the keyboard's power light on? If it is, check your screen. Is there something that's preventing you from typing? Maybe a dialogue box that wants an answer? If the light isn't on, continue down this list*
- *Check the plugs. Maybe the cord that connects the keyboard to the computer is loose or fell out.*
- *Reboot. Sometimes the stuff in the computer's boot-up sequence that makes the keyboard work gets lost. Restart your computer so it can re-establish itself.*
- *Do you eat at your keyboard? Doesn't everyone? I say this next solution hesitantly: Bang on the keys. Sometimes they get food between them and get stuck. If that doesn't work, turn the keyboard over and see what falls out.*

None of those work? Throw the darn thing out the window and buy a new one. They don't cost much anymore.

About the Authors

Structured Learning IT Team *is the premier provider of technology instruction books and ebooks to education professionals. Technology and keyboarding curriculums, how-to books, tips and tricks, a one-of-a-kind blog-based helpline—all the tools required to fulfill the tech needs of the 21st century classroom. All materials are classroom-tested, teacher-approved with easy-to-understand directions supported by online materials, websites, blogs, and wikis. Whether you are a new teacher wanting to do it right or a veteran educator looking for updated materials,* ***Structured Learning*** *and its team of technology teachers is there to assist you.*

Ask a Tech Teacher *is an award-winning resource* ***blog*** *run by a group of technology teachers. It has more than 60,000 visitors a month in search of resources and advice, offers oodles of free lesson plans, pedagogical conversation, website reviews and more. Its free newsletters and website articles are read by thousands, including teachers, homeschoolers, and anyone serious about finding the best way to maneuver the minefields of technology in education.*

Jacqui Murray *(lead Ask a Tech Teacher blogger) is the editor of SL's technology curriculum for K-sixth grade, creator of two technology training books for middle school, and four ebooks on technology in education. She is the author of* ***Building a Midshipman****, the story of her daughter's journey from high school to United States Naval Academy. She is webmaster for six blogs, an Amazon Vine Voice book reviewer, a columnist for Examiner.com, Editorial Review Board member for Journal for Computing Teachers, Cisco guest blogger, IMS tech expert, and a bi-weekly contributor to Write Anything. Her technology articles have appeared in hundreds of online newspapers and magazines.*

Kindergarten Keyboarding

KINDERGARTEN

OVERVIEW

Mouse mastery first, then an introduction to keyboarding where the focus is on key placement and posture

Objectives and Steps

_____Introduce technology. Ask students about their experiences with technology. Who has a computer? What do they use it for? What do their siblings/parents use it for?

_____Review parts of the computer—mouse, keyboard, headphones, mic, monitor, CPU, ports.

_____Explain that both the mouse and keyboard are input devices. Training will start with the mouse and move to keyboard.

_____Mouse use for new computer students isn't intuitive. Understanding requires explanation and reinforcement. Encourage students to be risk takers in these early stages.

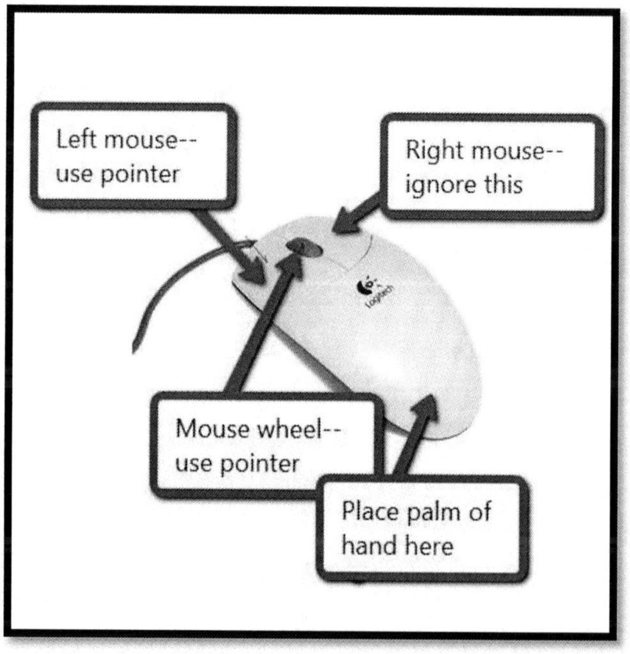

_____Demonstrate the correct way to hold the mouse: 1) the pointer (index finger) is on the left mouse button, 2) the middle finger is on the right mouse button, 3) thumb is on left side of mouse, 4) palm is on bottom of mouse. Walk around and make sure students are holding the mouse correctly.

_____Be sensitive to the fact that kindergartners barely know right from left. If they get it wrong, correct gently. I often say, "The other left" to indicate the other side.

_____Show students how their station is set up: 1) keyboard directly in front of them, directly in front of the monitor, one inch from table's edge, 2) mouse to the right of the keyboard, 3) chair one hand's width from table. See next pages for wall chart discussing proper position at the computer.

_____Left handed students may use the mouse traditionally or you may set it up to the keyboard's left. Find out what parents do at home and synchronize (see Articles for a discussion on lefties and mouse use).

_____Discuss mouse buttons. Have students click the left one. Discuss what that does and when it's used.

_____Have them click the right button on a program (maybe the internet). It drops down a menu with lots of words. Let them know they won't use this until next year or later.

_____Experiment with the mouse wheel. It rolls. Put in on a webpage and see how to go up and down the screen. Relate that to the scroll bar on the right side of the screen.

_____Explain terminology for mouse skills and try out each skill: 1) click means push left mouse button, 2) right-click means click right mouse button (again, they won't need that skill this year), 3) scroll means roll the mouse wheel and move up and down the page, 4) drag-and-drop means click the left mouse button and move the mouse.

_____Skills to be learned this year on mouse (see wall chart at end of unit):

- *Correct hand position (see inset)*
- *Left mouse button*
- *Ignore right mouse button*

Best Practices

- *Develop good mouse skills (skip right mouse button) before starting keyboarding*
- *In general, students should learn to type as fast as they need to for classwork. In kindergarten, there's no need for speed. It's about creating good habits*
- *Every time students type—in tech class and all classes--use good posture, proper hand position. Create good habits.*
- *Teach age-appropriate keyboard shortkeys*

- *Single click*
- *Double-click*
- *Click-drag-drop*
- *Mouse wheel*

_____As soon as students sit down to use their computer station, start on problem solving. Yes, it takes longer to teach them how to fix their volume control, but it takes shorter in the long-run. They feel good about their skills. They remember more than you expect. They use it at home which impresses parents with your genius (OK, yes, that's secondary).

_____Introduce the internet. Students will use it to visit some great mouse websites, but first, notice a few things:

- *Website address*
- *Tabs on browser—keeps track of open websites*
- *Screen—shows the page, but only part*
- *Scroll bar on right side and bottom—shows rest of page*
- *Links on page; what do they look like?*
- *Ads—discuss these and how to avoid them.*

_____Every time kindergartners visit the internet, review these basics until you are sure they understand.

_____Here are websites to start students on mouse skills (click or Google name). Spend twenty minutes per class for 3-4 classes on these while you troll the room and make sure hand and body positions are correct.

- More Mouse Skills
- Bees and Honey
- Mouse Song
- Mouse Use Video
- Mouse—Tidy Classroom
- Mouse—Wack a Gopher
- Mousing Around
- Single click to clean up the yard
- Mousing Around
- Mouse Program

_____Spend **Month #1** on mouse skills. Use keyboard only for nominal skills required to use mouse (like log-in).

_____Teach drag-and drop with 1) KidPix or Paint, and 2) puzzle programs like the following:

- Drag-drop games
- Drag and drop puzzles
- Drag and drop skills
- Great games for drag and drop
- Jigsaw puzzles
- Jigzone—puzzles

____**Month #2**, introduce typing, starting with a visual stroll around the keyboard. Point out key names, locations. Discuss some keys they'll need immediately like spacebar and shift.

____Before proceeding, gather students on the class rug and do finger exercises to encourage use of all fingers.

____Move to seats and discuss good posture. Here are suggestions:

- Keep keyboard in front of student and mouse to right (or left for lefties). Students want to push the keyboard out of the way so they can concentrate on the mouse. Don't let them. Make it a habit to keep the keyboard centered in front of their body with mouse comfortably to side
- Keep elbows tucked into their sides
- Keep hands curled like cat paws while typing
- Keep feet forward
- Keep both hands on keyboard, resting on home row
- Use right thumb for space bar

____Walk around the classroom (have parent helpers assist to make this go faster) and check to be sure all key points are followed.

____Start on an age-appropriate keyboarding program like Type to Learn Jr. or use an online keyboard program like Learn to Type, Alphabet rain game, Barracuda game, or Bubbles game (if you didn't purchase the pdf of this book with embedded links, simply Google these games and you'll find their online address. Alternatively, visit Ask a Tech Teacher, Great Websites tab, and you see these and more.). Rotate these programs throughout the year so students don't get tired of any one.

____If students have difficulty remembering right and left (as kindergartners often do), put a colored dot on their hands to coincide with the Type to Learn Jr. hand colors. Show them the relationship. Or, if you're using a different age-appropriate program, put a dot on the left hand to remind them—*the one with the dot is left.*

____**Month #3,** introduce Brown Bear typing. This program concentrates on **letter location only**. Explain that once students start remembering key placement, they'll get faster at all keyboarding. Have students use this program a few times a month in place of Type to Learn Jr.

____Here's how I use Brown Bear:

- *I set a goal for students (say, 28 points) that they must reach before moving on to whatever the next activity is in class.*

- *Every five minutes, I lower that goal so eventually all students achieve it.*
- *I continually remind them that this is all about remembering where the keys are.*
- *I give a crown to each student who beats the fastest score in the grade level for the year. For example, last year, our top score got to 46, with five crowns awarded throughout the year!*

_____My students tolerate TTL Jr. and love Brown Bear. Often, when it's free choice time, they select this online program.

_____Another program that reinforces mouse skills is Google Earth. To use it correctly, students must learn:

- How to click-drag the globe to move around
- How to use the mouse wheel to zoom in
- How to double-click a location to visit it

_____Other keys kindergartners should become familiar with through the typing program are:

- *Shift*
- *Caps lock*
- *Escape*
- *The F row*
- *Backspace*
- *Delete*

_____**Month #4-10**, use keyboarding in inquiry-driven projects that support classroom units. Have students use mouse skills for drawing pictures, type their names and short sentences, and use authentic class-inspired websites. This can be done in conjunction with:

- KidPix (or the free download TuxPaint)—combine art with text
- Geogreeting—find letters around the world
- Kerpoof
- Starfall
- Make a Story

_____Hands down, the following are the most common mistakes students make that prevent them from excelling at keyboarding. Besides good tips, these are a different way of saying things, for those multi-disciplinary students:

- Tuck elbows against the sides of body. This keeps hands in the right spot—on home row
- Use thumb for space bar. That leaves hands on home row
- Curl fingers over home row—they're cat paws, not dog paws
- Use inside fingers for inside keys, outside fingers for outside keys

- Use finger closest to the key you need. Sounds simple, but this isn't what usually happens with beginners.
- Keep pointers anchored to f and j
- Play keyboard like a piano (or violin, or guitar, or recorder). You'd never use pointer for all keys
- Fingers move, not hands. Hands stay anchored to f and j keys.
- Don't use caps lock for capitals! Use shift.

_____As the year progresses, reinforce student-centered problem-solving. This empowers them, gives them confidence and independence, and prevents boredom as they wait for Someone Else to solve their problems. They will use it at home which impresses parents with your genius (OK, that's secondary, but nice) Here are good starting points:

- *Double click doesn't work—push enter*
- *Volume doesn't work—check plugs*
- *Monitor doesn't work—check power*
- *Computer doesn't work—check power*

_____A typical keyboarding lesson for Kindergarten goes like this:

- Out of the 45 minutes a week you allocate to keyboarding, devote 10-15 minutes to keyboarding. Leave the rest to collaborate with class units of inquiry using keyboarding and mouse skills
- Mix up the 10-15 minutes with the following:
    - *Mouse skills*
    - *Keyboarding practice*
    - *Finger warm-up drills*
    - *Reinforcement of key placement with websites that concentrate on key placement, i.e., Brown Bear Typing*

_____**Extension**: Have students independently go to some of the websites you've suggested..

_____**Trouble shooting**: Spend time during each lesson correcting hand position on the mouse. It'll become a habit, but not right away.

Need help? Go to http://askatechteacher.com

SCOPE AND SEQUENCE CHECK LIST

Mouse

____*Proper hand position on mouse*
____*Click, hold, drag*
____*Double click*
____*Use of left button*

Problem-solving

____*Double click doesn't work—push enter*
____*Volume doesn't work—check plugs*
____*Monitor doesn't work—check power*
____*Computer doesn't work—check power*

Posture

____*Keyboard one inch off edge of table*
____*Correct posture—legs in front, body in front, elbows at sides*
____*Hands curled over keyboard (not flat)*
____*Keep feet flat on the floor*
____*Sit straight, body centered, hands on homerow*

Keyboarding

____*Use proper log-on/log-off procedures with help*
____*Demonstrate proper care and handling of keyboard, mouse*
____*Find period key*
____*Find Shift and Caps lock*
____*Difference between Shift and Caps lock*
____*Difference between backspace and delete*
____*Find Escape and Spacebar*
____*Use right thumb to key spacebar*
____*Place hands on home row keys*
____*Use both hands on keyboard, on their own sides*
____*Learn two basic keyboard shortcuts (Alt+F4, Esc)*
____*Use lab software for keyboarding*
____*Use internet-based sites for keyboarding*
____*Key in student's name*
____*Key in full sentences with proper grammar*

Put this on your wall:

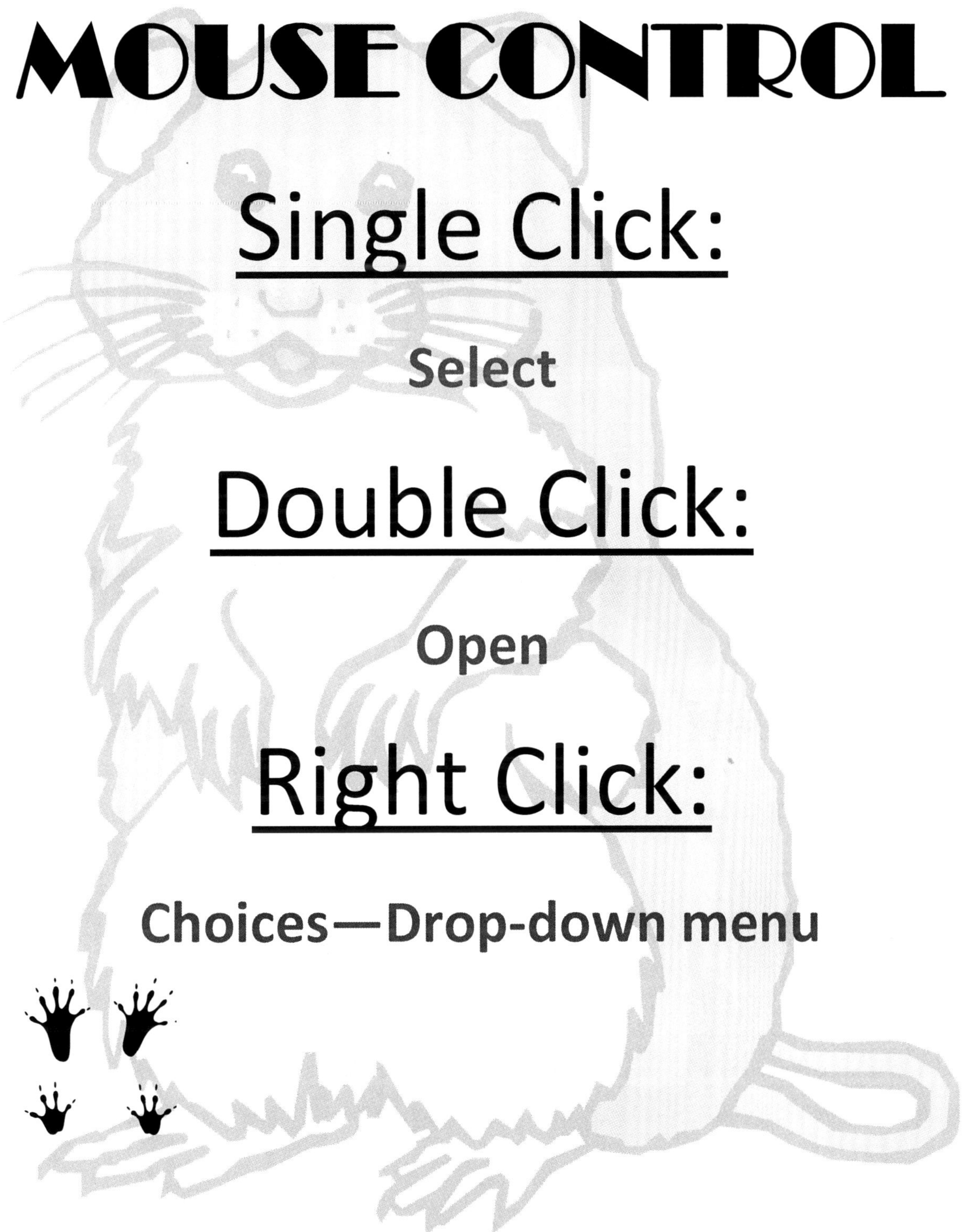

MOUSE CONTROL

Single Click:

Select

Double Click:

Open

Right Click:

Choices—Drop-down menu

Assume the Position

- Center legs in front of body
- Center body in front of keyboard
- Hands curved over home row
- Document to left of computer
- Use right thumb for space bar
- Eyes on screen

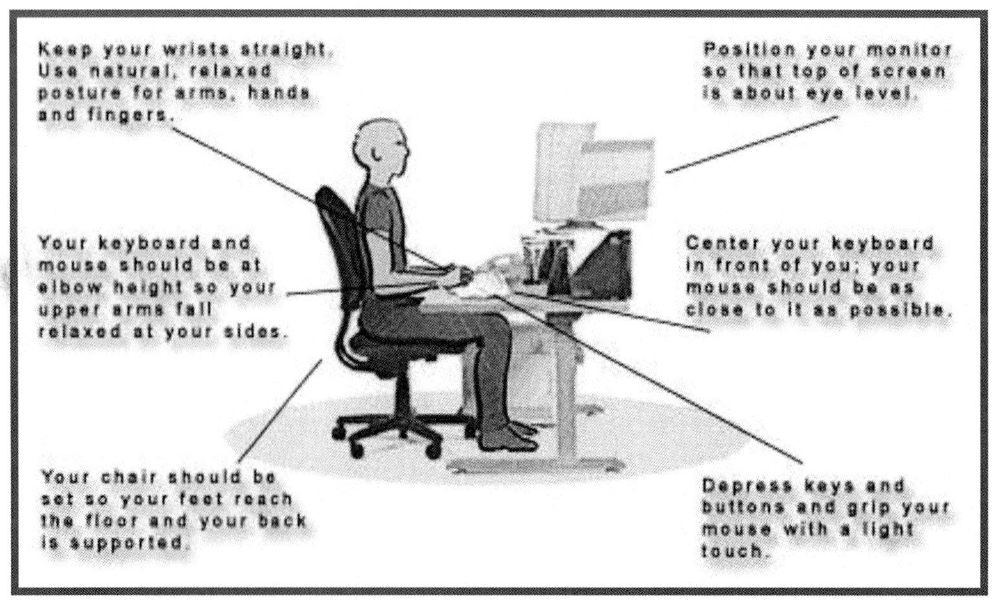

Great Keyboarding Hints for K-2

1. Make sure keyboard remains in centered front of student, mouse to right (or left for lefties). Students will push keyboard away to concentrate on mouse. Don't let them.
2. Have student tuck their elbows against the sides of their bodies. This keeps hands in the right spot—home row
3. Use thumb for space bar. That leaves hands on home row
4. Curl fingers over home row—they're cat paws, not dog paws
5. Use inside fingers for inside keys, outside for outside keys
6. Use finger closest to the key you need. Sounds simple, but this isn't what usually happens with beginners.
7. Keep pointers anchored to f and j
8. Play keyboard like a piano (or violin, or guitar, or recorder). You'd never use the pointer for all keys
9. Fingers move, not hands. Anchor hands to f and j keys
10. Don't use caps lock for capitals! Use shift.
11. Students must keep hands to themselves. Don't touch others mouse, keyboard, monitor. This gives them a sense of responsibility over their own station, knowing no one can touch it but them
12. Extra: Add a barrier. That reminds students to stay on the correct side of the keyboard

First Grade Keyboarding

FIRST GRADE

OVERVIEW

Mouse mastery and introduction to keyboarding with a focus on key placement and posture

Objectives and Steps

_____Introduce 'technology'—what's that mean? What's a computer (all the parts, not just the keyboard or monitor)? Ask students about their experiences. Who has their own computer? What do they use it for? What do their siblings/parents use it for? What do they remember from last year?

_____Review parts of the computer—mouse, keyboard, headphones, mic, monitor, CPU, plug-ins for parts, USB ports. Ask students for input. Let them show their knowledge of what was learned last year.

_____Remind first graders of the correct way to hold the mouse: 1) the pointer (index finger) is on the left mouse button, 2) the middle finger is on the right mouse button, 3) thumb is on left side of mouse, and 4) palm is on bottom of mouse.

_____Walk around the classroom (have parent helpers assist to make this go faster) and check to be sure all key points are followed.

_____Be sensitive to the fact that some students may still not know right from left. If they get it wrong, correct gently. I often say, "The other left" to indicate the other side.

_____Ask students to notice how their station is set up: 1) keyboard directly in front of them, directly in front of the monitor, one inch from edge of desk, 2) mouse to the right of the keyboard.

_____If any students are left handed, do they use the mouse the traditional way or do they want it set up on the left side of the keyboard? Find out what parents do at home and synchronize.

_____Review terminology for mouse skills:

- *Click*
- *Double click*
- *Right click (they won't need that this year)*
- *Scrolling*
- *Click-drag-drop*

_____**Month #1**, introduce the internet. Students will use it to visit some great mouse websites, but first, notice a few things:

- *Website address*
- *Tabs on browser—keeps track of open websites*
- *Screen—shows the page, but only part*
- *Scroll bar on right side and bottom—shows rest of page*
- *Links on page; what do they look like?*
- *Ads—discuss these and how to avoid them.*

Best Practices

- *Develop good mouse skills (skip right mouse button) before keyboarding*
- *In general, students need to type as fast as required for classwork. In first grade, there's no need for speed. It's about creating good habits*
- *Every time students type—in all classes--use good posture, hand position. Create good habits.*
- *Teach age-appropriate keyboard shortkeys*

_____Here are some great websites to review mouse skills (click the link or Google the name). Students will remember favorites from last year (Mouse Song, Bees and Honey). I spend twenty minutes per class, for 2-3 classes on this while I troll the room and make sure hand positions are correct.

- More Mouse Skills
- Bees and Honey
- Mouse Song
- Mouse Use Video
- Mouse—Tidy the Classroom
- Mouse—Wack a Gopher
- Mousing Around

- Single clicks to clean up the yard
- Mousing Around
- Mouse Program

_____See kindergarten pages for wall chart discussing mouse skills.

_____**Month #2**, reinforce drag-and drop skills with 1) KidPix or Paint (both drawing programs), and 2) puzzle programs like:

- Drag and drop games—visual
- Drag and drop puzzles
- Drag and drop skills
- Games for drag and drop
- Jigsaw puzzles
- Jigzone—puzzles

_____Can't use the links? Visit Ask a Tech Teacher, Great Websites tab, First Grade. You'll see these and more.

_____Another program that reinforces mouse skills is Google Earth. To use it correctly, students must know:

- *How to click-drag the globe to move around*
- *How to use the mouse wheel to zoom in*
- *How to double-click a location to visit it*

_____Circle Google Earth back to a classroom unit of inquiry. Focus on student mouse use while they enjoy exploring our planet.

_____**Month #3**: Before beginning keyboard practice, do finger exercises to encourage use of all fingers. These show students that they have eight fingers, all work, and some are stronger than others. Here's a link to fun exercises first graders love: http://learnkeyboarding.wikispaces.com/Keyboarding+Warm-ups.

_____Next, discuss basics of posture (see inset):

- *Make sure keyboard in front of student and mouse to the right (or left for lefties). Students want to push keyboard out of the way so they can concentrate on the mouse. Don't let them.*
- *Sit straight, centered to keyboard, feet flat on floor, about one hand's width from table*
- *Keep keyboard about one inch from edge of table*
- *Keep elbows tucked into sides*

- *Keep fingers slightly curved (think cat claws, not dog paws)*
- *Keep feet forward (first graders like to sit on their feet!)*
- *Keep both hands on keyboard, resting on home row*

_____If this is the first keyboard class, take a tour of the keyboard. Point out:

- *Enter—what's this used for?*
- *Space bar—it's use?*
- *Caps lock and shift—what's the difference?*
- *Backspace and delete—what's the difference?*
- *Tab—what's this used for?*
- *Home row—why is this row more important than others?*
- *Top row with numbers*
- *Ctrl, Alt keys—share some uses of these two keys (Alt+F4 to exit a program; Ctr+Alt+Del to log-onto the computer)*

_____Review keyboard technique as first graders practice typing:

- *Use right thumb for space bar*
- *Anchor pointers to f and j*
- *Play keyboard like a piano (or violin, or guitar, or recorder). You'd never use pointer for all keys*
- *Don't use caps lock for capitals! Use shift.*

_____First graders continue with Type to Learn Jr. or use an online keyboard program like Learn to Type, Alphabet rain game, Barracuda game, or Bubbles game (if you didn't purchase the pdf of this book with embedded links, simply Google these games and you'll find their online address. Alternatively, visit Ask a Tech Teacher, Great Websites tab, to find these and more.). Rotate programs throughout the year so students don't get tired of one.

_____Occasionally through the year (about once a month), have students use Brown Bear typing. This program concentrates on **letter location only**. Explain that once students remember key placement, they get faster at keyboarding.

_____Here's how I use Brown Bear:

- *I set a goal for students (say, 30 points) that they must reach before moving on to whatever the next activity is in class.*
- *Every five minutes, I lower that goal so eventually all students achieve it.*
- *I continually remind them that this is all about remembering where the keys are.*

- *I give a crown to each student who beats the fastest score in the grade level for the year. For example, last year, our top score got to 46, with five crowns awarded throughout the year!*

_____My students tolerate TTL Jr. and love Brown Bear. It is an oft-requested activity. Often, when it's free choice time, they select this program.

_____Other keys first graders should master through the typing program are:

- *Shift*
- *Caps lock*
- *Escape*
- *The F row*
- *Backspace*
- *Delete*

_____**Month #4-10,** use drawing programs like KidPix, TuxPaint, and/or Kerpoof to mix art and typing skills. Integrate a variety of projects throughout the year that support classroom discussion while encouraging good typing skills. As students work on a drawing, include typing—more and more as the year progresses:

- *Start with their name*
- *Next, add a phrase that doesn't require grammar (but does require spelling)*
- *Next, include a sentence that requires grammar*
- *By the end of the year, students can type 1-2 sentences with good grammar and spelling on a project. See next pages for examples (courtesy of Structured Learning First Grade Technology Curriculum)*

_____Keep keyboarding fun and light, but help students develop good habits they'll need when speed and accuracy become important.

_____As the year progresses, remind students to problem-solve. Ask who remembers how to fix the volume? The monitor? Knowing these solutions empowers them, gives them confidence and independence, and prevents boredom as they wait for Someone Else to help them. They feel good about their skills. Here are some good starting points:

- *Double click doesn't work—push enter*
- *Volume doesn't work—check plugs*
- *Monitor doesn't work—check power*
- *Computer doesn't work—check power*

_____When students are ready (midway-late in the year), move from Type to Learn Jr. to Type to Learn (or a similar progressive typing program used by your school). This I tell them is the 'big kids' program, one they'll use throughout Lower and Middle School. They love that.

_____A typical keyboarding lesson for first grade would go like this:

- You probably have 45 minutes a week set aside for keyboarding skills. Devote 15-25 minutes to keyboarding. Leave the rest to collaborate with classroom units of inquiry
- Mix up the 15-25 minutes with the following:
  - *Mouse skills*
  - *Keyboarding skills with software practice*
  - *Finger warm-up drills*
  - *Reinforce key placement with software/websites that concentrate only on key placement, i.e., Brown Bear Typing*

____**Extension**: Set up several of the online typing programs on different computers throughout the lab. Have students spend ten minutes at each station, then switch to a new program.

____**Trouble shooting**: Spend time during each lesson correcting hand position on the mouse. It'll become a habit, but not right away.

____**Trouble shooting**: Students can't use the right finger for the right key. *I wouldn't expect them to in first grade. Concentrate on posture, hands on keyboard, elbows at their sides. Worry about correct fingers in third grade.*

Need help? Go to http://askatechteacher.com

Notes

____

____

____

____________________________________.

SCOPE AND SEQUENCE CHECKLIST

Mouse

____*Proper hand position on mouse*
____*Click, hold, drag*
____*Double click*
____*Use of left button*

Problem-solving

____*Double click doesn't work—push enter*
____*Volume doesn't work—check plugs*
____*Monitor doesn't work—check power*
____*Computer doesn't work—check power*

Posture

____*Keyboard one inch off edge of table*
____*Correct posture—legs in front, body in front, elbows at sides*
____*Keep feet flat on the floor*
____*Sit straight, body centered, hands on homerow*
____*Hands curled over keyboard (not flat)*
____*Elbows at sides*

Keyboarding

____*Use proper log-on/log-off procedures.*
____*Demonstrate proper care and handling of keyboard, mouse*
____*Find period key*
____*Find Shift key and Caps lock key*
____*Difference between backspace, delete*
____*Escape, spacebar*
____*Use thumb to key space bar*
____*Rest fingers on home row keys*
____*Rest pointers on f and j*
____*Use both hands on keyboard, on their own sides*
____*Learn two basic keyboard shortcuts (Alt+F4, Esc)*
____*Use lab software for keyboarding*
____*Use internet-based sites for keyboarding*
____*Key in student's name*
____*Key in full sentences with proper grammar*

Project-based Keyboarding

(Courtesy of Structured Learning First Grade Technology Curriculum)

Second Grade Keyboarding

SECOND GRADE

OVERVIEW

Introduction to keyboarding with focus on key placement, posture, and two-hand position

Objectives and Steps

_____Keyboarding is a cumulative skill. What can be effectively learned in one grade depends heavily upon what is learned in earlier years. If hunt 'n peck habits become ingrained, it's difficult to develop keyboarding competence when it matters in later years.

_____Take one class session to review mouse skills—how to hold the mouse, single and double-clicks, scrolling, hand position with palm at bottom and thumb on left side. Grab a few mouse websites from Kindergarten and First Grade (refer back to those units in this book) and let students run through them as reminders.

_____During the first keyboard class of the year, tour the keyboard. Review:

- *Caps lock and shift—what's the difference?*
- *Backspace and delete—what's the difference?*
- *Tab—what's this used for?*
- *Home row—why is this row more important that the others?*
- *Top row with numbers*
- *Numeric keypad—works for numbers if NumLock invoked*
- *Ctrl, Alt keys—share some uses of these two keys (Alt+F4 to exit a program; Ctr+Alt+Del to log-onto the computer)*

_____Start with finger warm-ups. These show students that they have eight fingers, that all of them work, and that some are stronger than others.

Go to (http://learnkeyboarding.wikispaces.com/Keyboarding+Warm-ups) for fun exercises second graders love.

_____Do these exercises a couple times a month for about five minutes before starting keyboard practice.

_____Have students sit at keyboard using proper posture:

- *Back straight, feet flat, body centered in front of keyboard one hand's width from table*
- *Elbows close to sides*
- *Fingers slightly curved*
- *Hands on their own side of the keyboard*

_____Walk around the classroom (have parent helpers assist to make this go faster) and check to be sure all key points are followed.

_____No later than **Month #2** (it may take a bit to get through technology start-up), begin a progressive program of typing, such as purchased software like Type to Learn or a free online keyboarding program like Typing Web, TuxTyping, or Learn to Type—Brown Bear (if you didn't purchase the pdf of this book with embedded links, Google these names to find their address).

_____The goal for second grade is to reinforce skills learned last year and begin a focus on using all fingers.

- *Keep thumb on space bar*
- *Keep pointers anchored to f and j*
- *Play keyboard like a piano (or violin, or guitar, or recorder). You'd never use pointer for all keys*
- *Move fingers, not hands*
- *Don't use caps lock for capitals! Use shift.*

_____Remind students they have eight fingers and two thumbs—not just two pointers that hunt and peck.

Best Practices

- *In general, students should learn to type as fast as they need to for classwork. In second grade, there's no need for speed. It's about good habits*
- *Review good mouse skills*
- *Begin to use all fingers when typing*
- *Every time students type, use good posture, proper hand position. Create good habits.*
- *Teach typing with project-based lessons*
- *Work on age-appropriate keyboard shortkeys*

_____Don't discuss speed. Focus on posture, hand position, use of all fingers. These will eventually allow for speedy, accurate typing.

_____As students practice typing, anecdotally observe their posture for key points mentioned earlier in this unit. If possible, have parent helpers there to assist. Help them correct deficiencies. Take a moment to explain if need be.

_____Typing is best learned in projects that collaborate with classroom learning and require the use of keyboarding. No later than **Month #3**, begin a series of project-based typing activities using KidPix (or free alternatives like TuxPaint or Kerpoof). These will provide an authentic framework for learning typing as they integrate typing into classroom inquiry. These can be short reports, a letter, a story—pick one that works for your school environment.

_____Start with KidPix (or TuxPaint or Kerpoof). These programs were introduced in Kindergarten, reinforced in First Grade, and should be a comfortable approach to ramping up typing requirements. Pick differentiated projects that integrate technology AND require a nominal amount of typing. In second grade, this includes full sentences with good grammar and spelling. See the end of unit for examples (courtesy of the Structured Learning Second Grade Technology Curriculum).

_____By **Month #4**, introduce students to MS Word. Explain this is a program used throughout school. Ask them how many have sisters, parents who use it. What have they seen them do with it?

_____Before beginning, review the layout of the opening screen—the typing canvas, ribbons, cursor. Review some of the ways typing in Word is different from typing in KidPix.

- *typing begins where cursor is*
- *students don't push return at the end of a line (Word goes to the next line for you with what is called 'word wrap')*
- *Show-hide tool can be used to view returns, tabs, and spaces*

_____Start with a heading (name, teacher, date).

_____Change font to 48; type two-three sentences, each starting with capital letter and end with a period. Push the spacebar after every period and/or comma.

_____Correct red (spell-check) and green (grammar) squiggly lines

_____Feel free to add borders, images, WordArt, font colors and formatting (see example at end of unit). Punching all those letters in is hard and deserves a reward. Decorating is the fun part for young typists.

____Complete an MS Word project approximately **every two months**.

____**Throughout the year**, mix the use of progressive typing programs with game-type of programs. See "Online Keyboarding Programs for Second Graders" at the end of this lesson for ideas.

____**Consistently throughout the year**, introduce and reinforce the use of keyboard shortcuts (see "Shortkeys Second Graders Love" on next pages for age-appropriate shortkeys). These are quick two-key macros that accomplish commonly-performed tasks. For example:

- *When logging in, expect students to independently strike Ctr+Alt+Del and type in user name and password*
- *When unable to exit a program, expect students to try Alt+F4 before requesting assistance*
- *When saving, have students Ctrl+S*
- *When printing, have students Ctrl+P*
- *When needing to undo an action, Ctrl+Z (see poster at end of this lesson)*
- *When copying something, Ctrl+C*
- *When pasting something, Ctrl+V (Ask students why not Ctrl+P?)*
- *When adding a date, Shift+Alt+D*

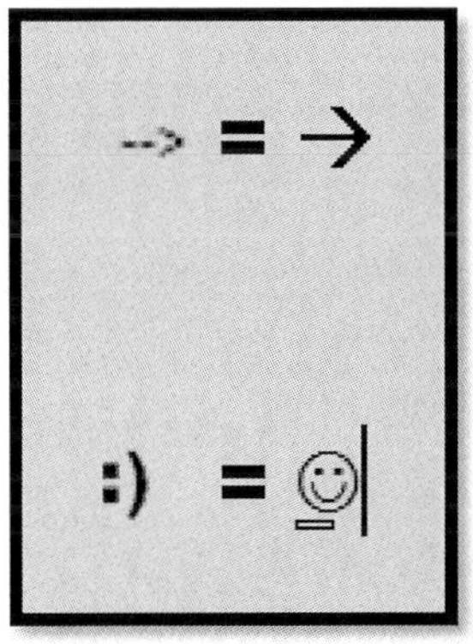

Students love to show off their techie-ness by using these and teaching them to others. See inset for two favorites.

____**Toward the end of the year** when students are comfortable with key placement, cover their hands with a cloth and start over on the keyboard, one row at a time. Dance Mat Typing is good for this, as are Nimble Fingers, Keyboard Practice, and Typing Practice. (If you don't have a PDF of this book, Google those names or go to Ask a Tech Teacher—Great Websites). Each of these focuses on one keyboard row at a time. I explain that in fourth and fifth grade, they type most of the time with hands covered. They love this--see it as a badge of honor to type with hands hidden. By the end of the year, home row is memorized, probably the QWERTY row and maybe even the lower row. It feels hard at first and quickly becomes easier.

____Keep keyboarding fun, but make sure students develop good habits. They'll need these when speed and accuracy become important.

____A typical keyboarding lesson for 2nd grade looks like this:

- Devote 10-15 minutes of the week's 45-minutes to keyboarding. Leave the rest to support classroom units of inquiry with projects that require typing (as noted earlier in this lesson)
- Mix up the 10-15 minutes with the following:
  - Keyboarding software practice
  - Online keyboarding websites
  - Finger practice
- Throughout all lessons, remind students of shortkeys that can accomplish oft-repeated activities like copy, paste, print, save, undo, etc.

_____**Extension**: Every time the class does an operation that can be performed with a shortkey, ask students who knows the shortkey for that function. For example, when inserting the date, ask who knows what the shortkey for that function is.

_____**Extension:** Any time students type, remind them that's the right time to focus on correct posture and hand position—nut just during keyboard practice time.

_____**Trouble shooting:** Students can't use the right fingers on the right keys (as is asked for in the programs). *Remind students they don't need to worry about this until next year.*

Need help? Go to http://askatechteacher.com

Notes

____

____

____

____

__________________.

SCOPE AND SEQUENCE CHECK LIST

Mouse

_____*Proper hand position on mouse*
_____*Click, hold, drag, double-click,*
_____*Use of left and right button*
_____*Use mouse wheel to scroll down pages*

Problem-solving

_____*Double click doesn't work—push enter*
_____*Volume doesn't work—check plugs*
_____*Monitor doesn't work—check power*
_____*Computer doesn't work—check power*
_____*Where's my program—check the taskbar*

Posture

_____*Keyboard one inch off edge of table*
_____*Correct posture—legs in front, body in front, elbows at sides*
_____*Feet flat on the floor*
_____*Body straight, centered, one hand's width from table edge*
_____*Hands curled over homerow (not flat)*

Keyboarding

_____*Use proper log-on/log-off procedures.*
_____*Demonstrate proper care and handling of keyboard, mouse*
_____*Find period, escape, tab,*
_____*Find Shift key and Caps lock key*
_____*Understand difference between backspace, delete*
_____*Understand purpose of cursor in typing*
_____*Use thumb to key space bar*
_____*Rest fingers on home row keys*
_____*Use both hands on keyboard, on their own sides*
_____*Learn seven basic keyboard shortcuts (Alt+F4, Esc, Ctrl+Z, Ctrl+P, Ctrl+S, Ctrl+C, Ctrl+V)*
_____*Use lab software and internet-based sites for keyboarding*
_____*Key in full sentences with proper grammar*
_____*Key paragraphs with tab to indent*

Online Keyboarding Programs for Second Graders

1. Alphabet rain game
2. Barracuda game
3. Bubbles game
4. Finger jig practice game
5. Free typing tutor
6. Keyboard challenge
7. Keyboard practice
8. Keyboard—free online course
9. Keyboarding practice
10. Keyboarding—games
11. Keyboarding—lessons
12. Keyboarding—lessons, quiz
13. Keyboarding—more lessons
14. Keyboarding—quick start
15. Keyboarding—speed quiz
16. Krazy keyboarding for kids
17. Online typing lessons
18. Typing Defense

Shortkeys Second Graders Love

Maximize window	Double click title bar
Quick Exit	Alt+F4
Date and Time	Shift+Alt+D = Date
	Shift+Alt+T = Time
Show taskbar	WK (Windows key)

Ctrl Key Combinations

CTRL+C: Copy	CTRL+K: Add hyperlink
CTRL+X: Cut	CTRL+E: Center align
CTRL+V: Paste	CTRL+L: Left align
CTRL+Z: Undo	CTRL+R: Right align
CTRL+B: Bold	CTRL+P: Print
CTRL+U: Underline	CTRL+ : Zoom in Internet
CTRL+I: Italic	CTRL- : Zoom out Internet
CTRL+P: Print	

Second Grade Typing Projects

Courtesy of the Structured Learning Second Grade Technology Curriculum

Put this sign on your walls to help with Windows basics:

UNDO

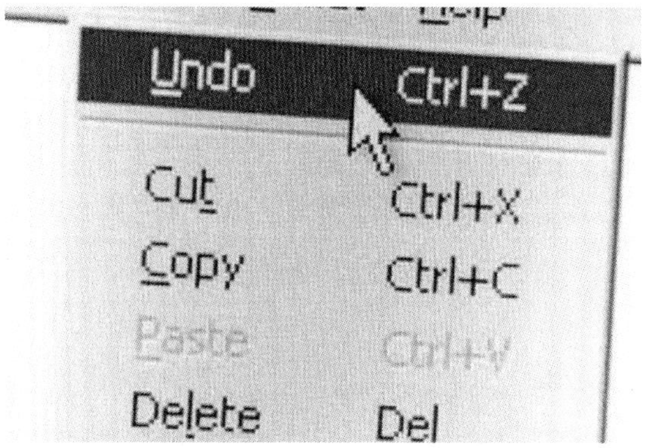

is your

Friend

Third Grade Keyboarding

Third GRADE

OVERVIEW

Reinforce basics of key position, posture and hand position. Begin accuracy and technique with grade-level goal of 15wpm

Objectives and Steps

_____Keyboarding is a cumulative skill. What can be effectively learned in one grade depends heavily upon what is learned in earlier years. If hunt 'n peck habits become ingrained, it's difficult to develop keyboarding competence when it matters in later years.

_____During the first keyboard class of the year, tour the keyboard. Review:

- *Caps lock and shift—what is the difference between these?*
- *Backspace and delete—what's the difference between these?*
- *Tab—what's this used for?*
- *Home row—why is this row more important than others?*
- *Top row with numbers*
- *Numeric keypad—works for numbers if NumLock invoked*
- *Ctrl, Alt keys—share some uses of these two keys (Alt+F4 to exit a program; Ctr+Alt+Del to log-onto the computer)*

_____Basics to remember during third grade are:

- *Keep fingers on home row keys*
- *Use correct posture for typing (see inset)*
    - *Sit up straight, shoulders back, head up, body centered in front of keyboard, feet flat on ground, body one hand's width from table*
    - *Keep elbows close to sides*
    - *Keep hands on their own side of the keyboard*

- *Have fingers slightly curved*
- *Place keyboard one inch from edge of table*

- *Begin focus on touch typing*
- *Use right thumb for spacebar*
- *Keep copy to the left or right of keyboard, eyes on copy or screen—NOT keyboard*
- *Key with a steady even pace*
- *Use keyboard shortcuts (i.e., Ctrl+B, Shift+Alt+D, Ctrl+Z)*
- *Apply keyboarding skills whenever possible, not just during typing practice*

_____I add two keyboarding hints in third grade that appeal to their more mature mind:

- *Use inside fingers for inside keys, outside for outside keys*
- *Use finger closest to the key you need. Sounds simple, but this isn't what usually happens with beginners.*

_____The focus in third grade moves from good habits (these are now established and simply need to be reinforced) to memorizing keys. Once students know key placement, speed and accuracy will come (don't worry if it doesn't happen until 5-8th grade. That's common).

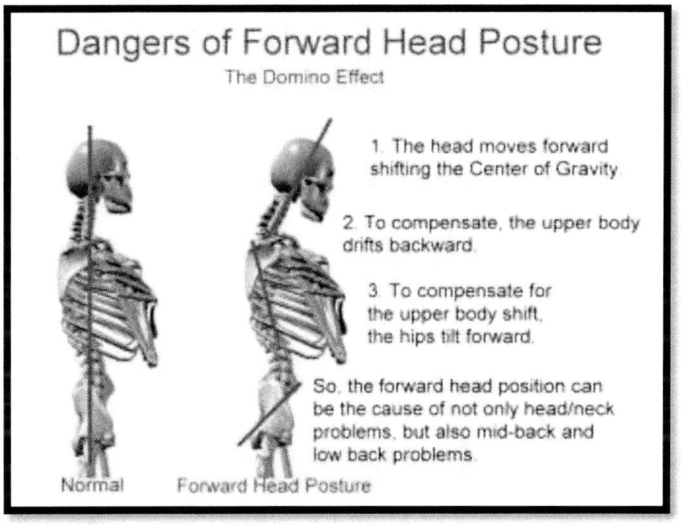

_____Start **Month #1** with five minutes of finger warm-ups and repeat these several times a month. These show students that they have ten fingers that work, even though some are stronger than others. Go to (http://learnkeyboarding.wikispaces.com/Keyboarding+Warm-ups) for fun exercises third graders love.

_____Start keyboard practice by working on one row at a time, one per month, using Dance Mat Typing and Nimble Fingers. Here's a schedule for Months **#1, #2, and #3**:

1) *first month: home row*
2) *second month: QWERTY row*
3) *third month: lower row*

_____During the first keyboarding session, walk around the classroom (have parent helpers assist to make this go faster) and check to be sure all key posture points are followed (see above).

_____Students practice 10-15 minutes during class time and 45 minutes per week as homework on this schedule of one row per month (see homework at end of Third Grade Unit).

_____Typing is best learned in projects that collaborate with classroom learning and require the use of keyboarding. No later than **Month #2**, begin a series of project-based typing using MS Word or Publisher (or similar). These will provide an authentic framework for learning keyboarding as students integrate it into classroom inquiry. These can be short reports, magazines, trifolds, a story—pick one that works for your school environment. Reinforce use of enter key to end paragraphs, word-wrap to go to next line, tab to indent, purpose of cursor in word processing. See the end of this unit for examples (courtesy of the Structured Learning Third Grade Technology Curriculum).

Best Practices

- *Students should learn to type as fast as they need to for classwork. Set a goal of 15wpm—about as fast as they handwrite.*
- *Start focusing on speed and accuracy while remembering good habits like proper hand and body positions.*
- *Use typing skills in classroom projects more often than last year*
- *Work on age-appropriate keyboard shortkeys*

_____**Each grading period**, students take a blank keyboard quiz (see end of unit for example) to test important keys (let students know that in 4/5th grade, they'll take a blank keyboard quiz that includes ALL keys). Students work in pairs to fill in all fifteen key names. This knowledge of key placement quickly translates to improved speed and accuracy.

_____**Each grading period,** students take a keyboard quiz to determine speed and accuracy (see sample on next pages. Or, use a few pages from a book students are reading.) As students take this quiz, anecdotally notice who is using all fingers and correct posture. Those that aren't, lose points.

_____After the quiz, allow one minute to correct spelling errors using a right-click on red squiggly lines.

_____The first quiz is the benchmark. The rest are graded based on improvement:

- *20% improvement* *10/10*

- *10-20% improvement* 9/10
- *1-10% improvement* 8/10
- *No improvement* 7/10
- *Slowed down* 6/10

_____Since third graders are barely into percents, we discuss the grading scale and use the conversation to support math concepts.

_____Grade level standards are:

3rd Grade: 15 wpm	*6th Grade: 35wpm*
4th Grade: 25 wpm	*7th Grade: 40 wpm*
5th Grade: 30 wpm	*8th Grade: 45 wpm*

_____Post a list of 'keyboard speedsters' on the bulletin board which includes all students who reached the grade level standard for speed and accuracy. You may decide to give them an award—something that works for your school. In my classes, students get a free dress pass (we are a uniform school).

_____**Month #4** (after study of all three keyboard rows is completed), students switch to Type to Learn (installed software) or Typing Web (online—free) for classtime practice and homework. By this time, students should have all keys memorized.

_____**Consistently throughout the year**, introduce and reinforce the use of keyboard shortcuts (see "Shortkeys Third Graders Love Using" on next pages for age-appropriate shortkeys). These are quick macros that accomplish commonly-performed tasks. For example:

- *When logging in, expect students to independently strike Ctr+Alt+Del and type in user name and password*
- *When unable to exit a program, expect students to try Alt+F4 before requesting assistance*
- *When saving, have students Ctrl+S*
- *When printing, have students Ctrl+P*
- *When needing to undo an action, remind students to try Ctrl+Z*
- *When copying something, Ctrl+C*
- *When pasting something, Ctrl+V (Ask students why not Ctrl+P?)*

Students love to show off their techie-ness by using these and teaching them to others.

_____Somewhere around **Month #6**, test students to determine who can type faster than they can handwrite. Do this by circling back on science class and the scientific method:

- Discuss whether students handwrite faster/slower than they type. Ask students to share thoughts on why their opinion is true. You are likely to get opinions on both sides of this discussion. If not, prod students with logic for both.

- Suggest an experiment to see which is faster—handwriting or typing.
- Start with a discussion on the Scientific Method, and then develop a hypothesis for this research, maybe: *Third grade students in Mr. X's class can handwrite faster than they type* (this is the most common opinion in my classes).
- Have them hand-copy the three-minute typing quiz they took earlier in the trimester.
- Analyze the results: Compare their handwriting speed to their typing speed.
- Discuss results: Why do students think some students typed faster and others typed slower? (In my classes, third graders typed approx. 10wpm and handwrote approx. 15wpm. Discussion was heated and enthusiastic on reasons. Especially valuable were the thoughts of those rare students who typed faster).

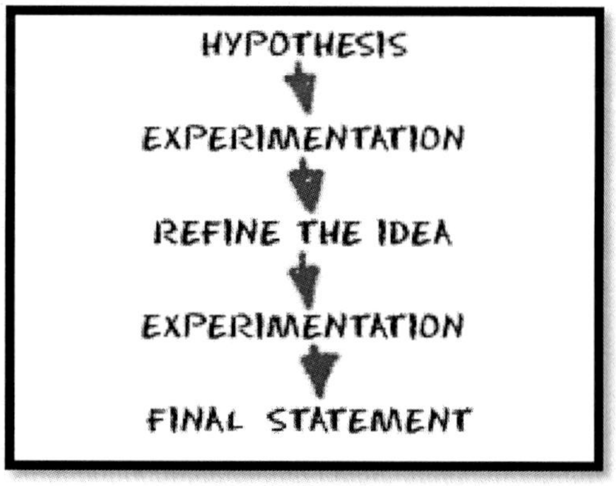

- Students will offer lots of reasons for slower typing (they're new to typing, don't do it much in class, their hands got off on the keyboard). One reason is that students don't usually type from copy. Key in on this reason (quite valid, I think—don't you?) and revise the experiment to have students type and handwrite from a prompt.
- What is the final conclusion?
- If possible, share results from 4-8th grade. What grade level do students consistently type faster than they handwrite? Why? Are students surprised by the answer?
- Post a list of students who type faster than they handwrite.
- *Note: There are varying examples of the scientific method when discussing the elementary grades. Talk to your science teacher and adapt this experiment to the one she uses.*

_____**Occasionally through the year**, have students use a program called TypingTest.com to see how speed and accuracy is progressing.

_____**Toward the end of the year** when students are comfortable with key placement, cover their hands with a cloth and start over on the keyboard, one row at a time. Dance Mat Typing is good for this, as are Nimble Fingers, Keyboard Practice, and Typing Practice. (If you don't have a PDF of this book, Google those names or go to Ask a Tech Teacher—Great Websites). Each of these focuses on one keyboard row at a time. I explain to students that in fourth and fifth grade, they type most of the time with hands covered. They love this--see it as a badge of honor to type with hands hidden. By the end of the year, home row is memorized, probably the QWERTY row and maybe even the lower row. It feels hard at first and quickly becomes easier.

_____Keep keyboarding fun, but help students develop good habits. They'll need these when speed and accuracy become necessary.

_____A typical keyboarding lesson for 3rd grade looks like this:

- Devote 10-15 minutes of each 45-minute session to keyboarding practice, reviewing homework that's due and coming up. Leave the rest to supporting classroom units of inquiry with projects that require typing (as noted earlier in this lesson)
- Mix up the 10-15 minutes with the following:
  - Keyboarding software practice
  - Online keyboarding websites
  - Finger practice
  - Typing Tests
- Throughout all lessons, remind students of shortkeys that can accomplish oft-repeated activities like copy, paste, print, save, undo.

_____**Extension**: At the end of the year, have a Team Challenge. Click here for example (scroll to Week 3) or go to next page for questions I use. Break class into teams. Ask a question from the list and give only three seconds to answer. They can answer verbally or with the correct finger. The focus is on speed—students must know the answers, not have to think about it.

_____**Trouble shooting**: I can't type with hands covered. *Keep practicing.*

Need Help? Go to http://askatechteacher.com

SCOPE AND SEQUENCE CHECK LIST

Problem-solving

_____*Double click doesn't work—push enter*

_____*Volume doesn't work—check plugs*

_____*Monitor doesn't work—check power*

_____*Keyboard doesn't work—check plugs, reboot*

_____*Computer doesn't work—check power*

_____*Difference between save and save-as*

_____*I deleted *** by accident—Ctrl+Z*

Posture

_____*Keyboard one inch off edge of table*

_____*Correct posture—legs in front, body in front, elbows at sides*

_____*Feet flat on the floor, body one hand's width from edge of table*

_____*Sit straight, body centered*

_____*Hands curled over homerow, on their own side of keyboard; fingers anchored on f and j*

Keyboarding

_____*Use proper log-on/log-off procedures.*

_____*Demonstrate proper care and handling of computer*

_____*Find escape, tab, Shift key, Caps lock, Alt, Ctrl, Esc, PrintScreen, F4*

_____*Know difference between backspace, delete*

_____*Understand purpose of cursor in typing*

_____*Use right thumb to key space bar*

_____*Learn ten basic keyboard shortcuts (Alt+F4, Esc, Ctrl+P, Ctrl+S, Ctrl+C, Ctrl+V, Ctrl+Alt+Del, double-click to enlarge window, Alt+Tab, ???)*

_____*Use lab software for keyboarding*

_____*Use internet-based sites for keyboarding*

_____*Key in full sentences with proper grammar*

_____*Key paragraphs with enter and tab to indent*

_____*Set keyboard goal of 15 wpm*

_____*Practice touch typing*

_____*Compose at the keyboard*

THIRD GRADE TYPING PROJECTS

Courtesy of the <u>Structured Learning Third Grade Technology Curriculum</u>

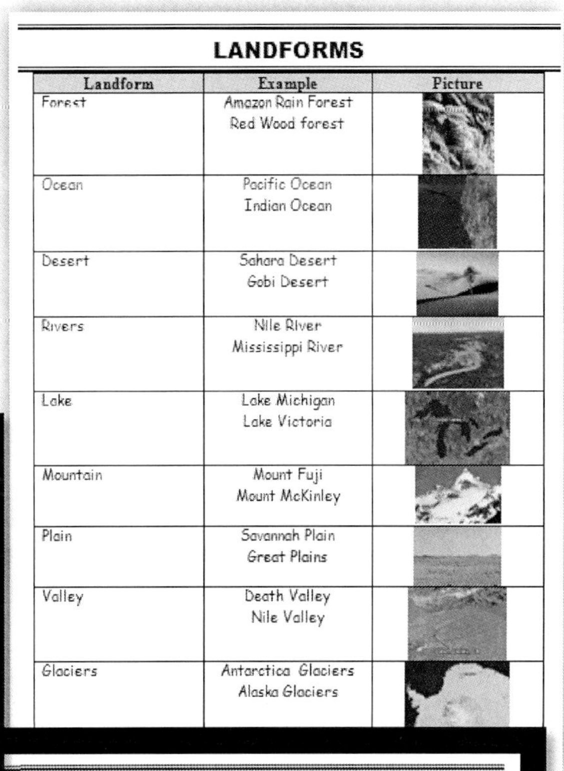
LANDFORMS

Landform	Example	Picture
Forest	Amazon Rain Forest Red Wood forest	
Ocean	Pacific Ocean Indian Ocean	
Desert	Sahara Desert Gobi Desert	
Rivers	Nile River Mississippi River	
Lake	Lake Michigan Lake Victoria	
Mountain	Mount Fuji Mount McKinley	
Plain	Savannah Plain Great Plains	
Valley	Death Valley Nile Valley	
Glaciers	Antarctica Glaciers Alaska Glaciers	

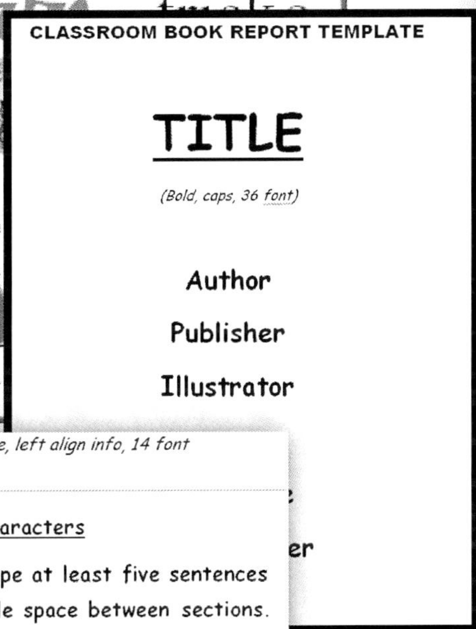
CLASSROOM BOOK REPORT TEMPLATE

TITLE

(Bold, caps, 36 font)

Author

Publisher

Illustrator

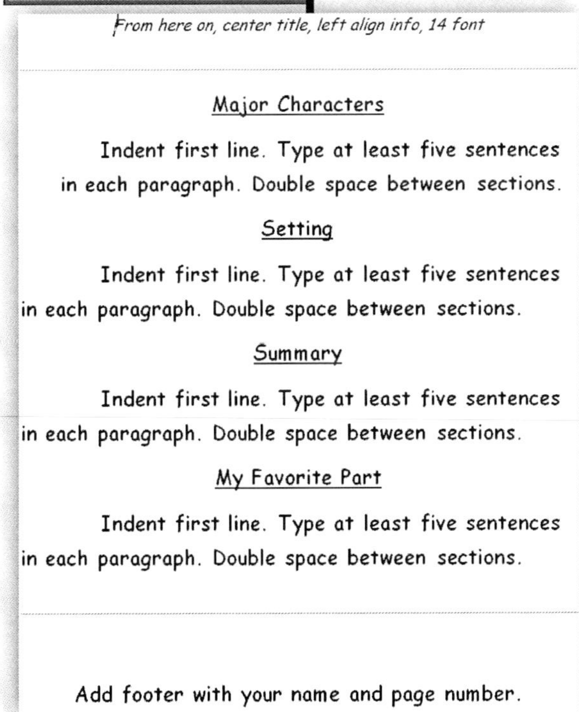
From here on, center title, left align info, 14 font

<u>Major Characters</u>

Indent first line. Type at least five sentences in each paragraph. Double space between sections.

<u>Setting</u>

Indent first line. Type at least five sentences in each paragraph. Double space between sections.

<u>Summary</u>

Indent first line. Type at least five sentences in each paragraph. Double space between sections.

<u>My Favorite Part</u>

Indent first line. Type at least five sentences in each paragraph. Double space between sections.

Add footer with your name and page number.

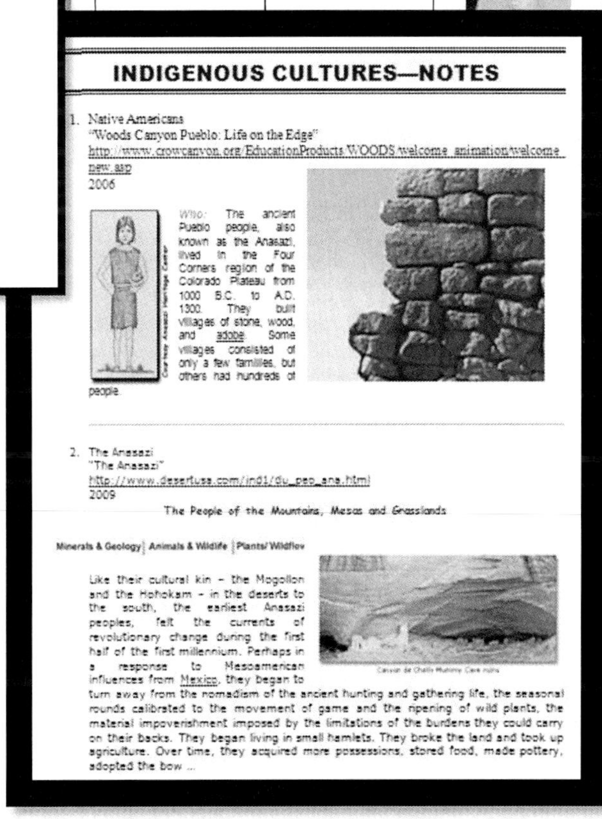
INDIGENOUS CULTURES—NOTES

1. Native Americans
"Woods Canyon Pueblo: Life on the Edge"
http://www.crowcanyon.org/EducationProducts/WOODS/welcome_animation/welcome_new.asp
2006

Who: The ancient Pueblo people, also known as the Anasazi, lived in the Four Corners region of the Colorado Plateau from 1000 B.C. to A.D. 1300. They built villages of stone, wood, and adobe. Some villages consisted of only a few families, but others had hundreds of people.

2. The Anasazi
"The Anasazi"
http://www.desertusa.com/ind1/du_peo_ana.html
2009

The People of the Mountains, Mesas and Grasslands

Minerals & Geology | Animals & Wildlife | Plants/Wildflov

Like their cultural kin – the Mogollon and the Hohokam – in the deserts to the south, the earliest Anasazi peoples, felt the currents of revolutionary change during the first half of the first millennium. Perhaps in a response to Mesoamerican influences from Mexico, they began to turn away from the nomadism of the ancient hunting and gathering life, the seasonal rounds calibrated to the movement of game and the ripening of wild plants, the material impoverishment imposed by the limitations of the burdens they could carry on their backs. They began living in small hamlets. They broke the land and took up agriculture. Over time, they acquired more possessions, stored food, made pottery, adopted the bow ...

KEYS THIRD GRADERS SHOULD KNOW

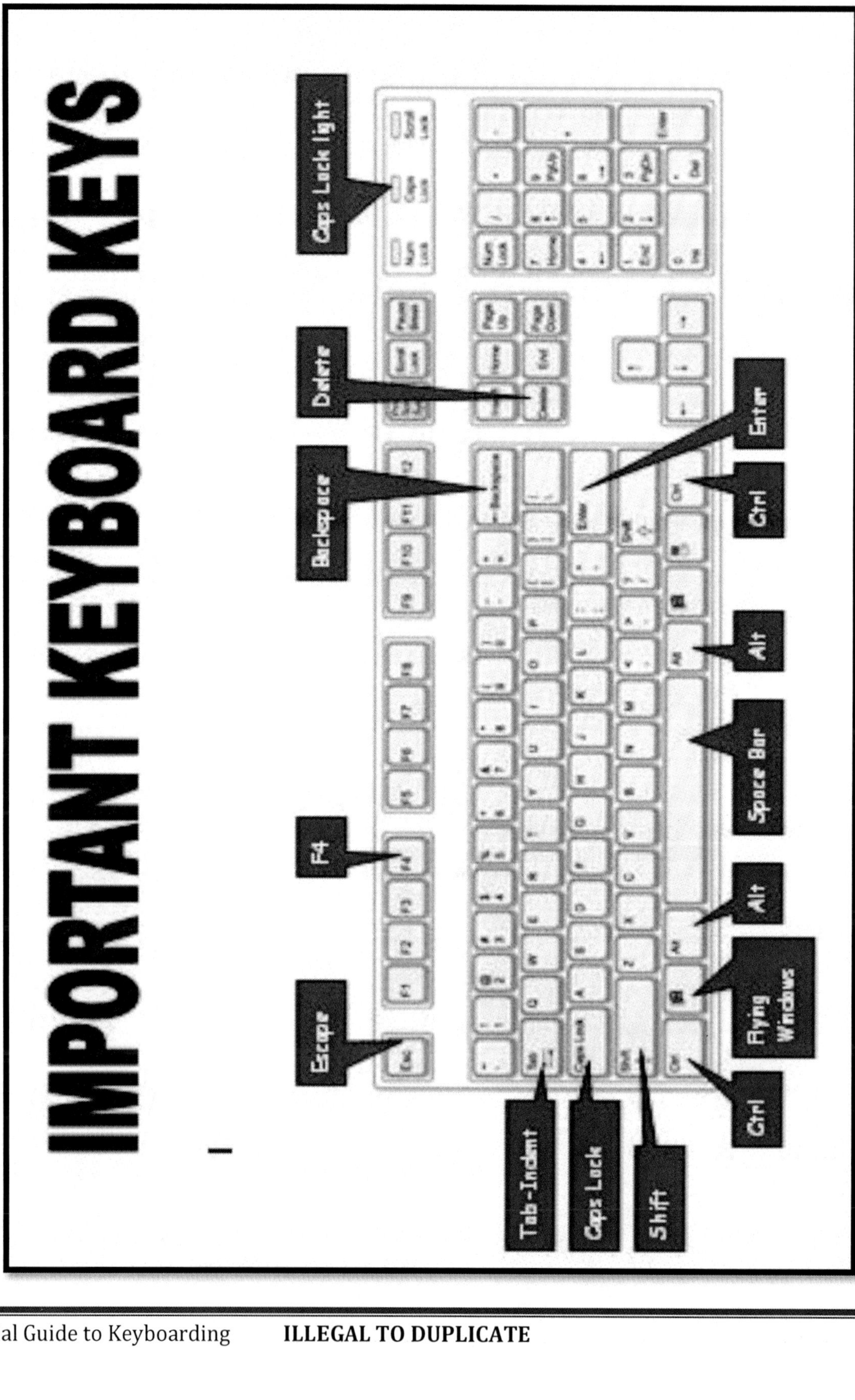

KEYS THIRD GRADERS SHOULD KNOW—TEST

SAMPLE KEYBOARD SPEED QUIZ

The Best Thing in the World

Once upon a time, four princes lived in a far away land. Their father was old. One day he said, "I will not live long now. Today you must start out into the world. In a year, bring back the best thing you have found. The one who can pick the best thing shall be my new king."

The first brother said he would look in every city or town to buy the best thing for his father." The next two brothers said they would both go on fast ships over the sea to find something better.

The last brother said, "I am going to ask the people here in our own land to tell me the best thing." The other three began to laugh. "Then you will never be king!" The last brother started off. When he had gone about six miles, he met a man. "What do you carry in those big bags?" he asked. "The best thing in the world," said the man. "These are full of good nuts which fall from my five trees."

"I don't think that would work," said the brother to himself, "I must try again."

He went another seven miles and found a small brown bird. It had been hurt, so he put it in his coat where it could keep warm. As he went on, he saw a girl crying. He ran to meet her.

"Why are you crying?" he asked the little girl.

"I want to get some water from the well," she said. "We use so much. We drink cold water. We wash the clothes clean with hot water. But I do not know how to pull it up. Please show me."

The brother said, "Hold this bird and I will help you. It does not fly around anymore because it got its wing hurt."

"Thank you. What a pretty bird!" she said. "I wish you would give it to me. If you will let me keep it, I will always be very kind to it. I will take care of it myself and make it grow well."

"Yes, you may have it," said the brother.

So he gave her the bird and went on. At night, he went to sleep under a round yellow haystack. When it was light again he walked on. Every day he would walk eight or ten miles. He asked the people about the best thing in the world. Some said it was best to sing. Some said it was best to run and jump and play. Some said the green grasses were best. Some liked the red and blue and white flowers best. One man said the best thing was to ride a black horse. The Prince always stopped to help people who needed it. Soon he made many friends. All the people began to like him. They would say, "See there goes the king's son. He would be just the right kind of king for us."

Every door was open to him. The people would call to him to stop. They would ask him to come and eat with them. After he ate, he would sit down and read to the children. After he read, he showed them how to draw and write. Months went by. He still had no beautiful thing to take to his father. Just before the year was done, he went home again. The time came went he king called his sons together.

"What did you bring?" He asked them all. The other brothers had many beautiful things.
"And what did you bring?" said the king to the last brother.

"This is too funny!" said the other brothers. "He has nothing!"

But the king was kind to the last brother. "What did you bring me?" the king asked again.

"I bring only the friendship of your people," said the last the brother.

"That is the best thing!" cried his father. "You shall be the new king."

This passage contains many of the 220 Dolch Basic Sight Words. Adapted from http://www.bristolvaschools.org/mwarren/DolchWords.htm

SHORTKEYS THIRD GRADERS LOVE USING

Maximize window	Double click title bar
Quick Exit	Alt+F4
Date and Time	Shift+Alt+D = Date Shift+Alt+T = Time
Show taskbar	WK (Windows key)
Shows desktop	WK+M

Ctrl Key Combinations

- CTRL+C: Copy
- CTRL+X: Cut
- CTRL+V: Paste
- CTRL+Z: Undo
- CTRL+B: Bold
- CTRL+U: Underline
- CTRL+I: Italic
- CTRL+P: Print
- CTRL+K: Add hyperlink
- CTRL+E: Center align
- CTRL+L: Left align
- CTRL+R: Right align
- CTRL+ : Internet zoom in
- CTRL- : Internet zoom out

Fun Keyboard Shortcuts:

<+=+> = ⇔

—+> = →   :+) = ☺

ANNUAL TEAM CHALLENGE—KEYBOARD

Review

Review the following concepts. These are similar to questions that will be asked during the upcoming Team Challenge to find the summer's most tech-savvy student!

1. What's the computer log in
2. What's the computer password
3. What's your password for TTL4
4. What row do your finger start on before you even type a letter
5. What's the row above home row
6. What's the row below home row called
7. How do you find the f and j key without looking
8. Name three keys you use your pinkie to push
9. Name three keys you use your ring finger to push
10. Name three keys you use your middle finger to push
11. Name three keys you use your pointer to push
12. Name one key you use your right thumb to push
13. Which finger do you use for the backspace key
14. Which finger do you use for the shift key
15. Which finger do you use for the enter key
16. Which finger do you use for the escape key
17. What are three rules of how you sit at the keyboard
18. Do you have cat's paws or dog paws at the computer
40. What is one keyboard shortcut
19. Why (do you use cat's paws or dog paws)
20. What part of the chair do you sit on when keyboarding
21. Where are your elbows when keyboarding
22. Where does your right thumb rest when keyboarding
23. What is typing without looking at the keys called
24. Which finger pushes the a key
25. Which finger pushes the b key
26. Which finger pushes the ac key
27. Which finger pushes the d key
28. Which finger pushes the e key
29. Which finger pushes the f key
30. Which finger pushes the g key
31. Which finger pushes the h key
32. Which finger pushes the i key
33. Which finger pushes the j key
34. Which finger pushes the k key
35. What finger pushes enter
36. What's the keyboard shortcut to exit a program
37. As a general rule, which finger pushes a key
38. How do you capitalize a letter
39. As a general rule, do you fingers move or your hands in finding the keys
41. What is a desktop

HOMEWORK—OCTOBER THROUGH MAY

October

Spend 15 minutes, four times a week, for the entire month, on DanceMat Typing (http://www.bbc.co.uk/schools/typing/)—homerow keys only. Repeat until you feel you have memorized key placement. Then, cover keys with a dish towel or a light cloth so you cannot see your hands. Do all exercises for the rest of the month with hands covered. The goal: to memorize location of keys without taking your eyes from the screen and improve speed and accuracy throughout the month.

On last day of month, submit your homework via dropbox (or email if dropbox not available). Write 3-5 sentences addressing on the following:

1. Verify you have completed this homework. That is, you typed 15 minutes 4 times a week (for one hour a week) for four weeks, for a total of four hours a month
2. Share what was easy/difficult
3. Reflect on how you see keyboarding affecting other classes, other homework assignments, life in general

November

Spend 15 minutes, four times a week, for the entire month, on DanceMat Typing (http://www.bbc.co.uk/schools/typing/)—only stages that cover homerow and QWERTY row (the row right above home row). Repeat until you feel you have memorized key placement. Then, cover keys with a dish towel or a light cloth so you cannot see your hands. Do all exercises for the rest of the month with hands covered. The goal: to memorize location of keys without taking your eyes from the screen and improve speed and accuracy.

On last day of month, submit your homework via dropbox (or email if dropbox not available). Write 3-5 sentences addressing on the following:

1. Verify you have completed this homework. That is, you typed 15 minutes 4 times a week (for one hour a week) for four weeks, for a total of four hours a month
2. Share what was easy/difficult
3. Reflect on how you see keyboarding affecting other classes, other homework assignments, life in general

December

Spend 15 minutes, four times a week, for the entire month, on DanceMat Typing (http://www.bbc.co.uk/schools/typing/) on homerow, QWERTY row and lower row (below home row). Repeat until you feel you have memorized key placement. Then, cover keys with a dish towel or a light cloth so you cannot see your hands. Do all exercises for the rest of the month with hands covered. The goal: to memorize location of keys without taking your eyes from the screen and improve speed and accuracy.

On last day of month, submit your homework via dropbox (or email if dropbox not available). Write 3-5 sentences addressing on the following:

1. Verify you have completed this homework. That is, you typed 15 minutes 4 times a week (for one hour a week) for four weeks, for a total of four hours a month
2. Tell me what was easy/difficult
3. Reflect on how you see keyboarding affecting other classes, other homework assignments, life in general

January

Spend 15 minutes, four times a week, for the entire month, on Type to Learn (or another typing program from appendix—NOT DanceMat Typing). Start with prequiz (if there is one) and progress through lessons. If you use TTL, the teacher can track progress.

On last day of month, submit your homework via dropbox (or email if dropbox not available). Write 3-5 sentences addressing on the following:

1. Verify you have completed homework. That is, you typed 15 minutes 4 times a week (for one hour a week) for four weeks, for a total of four hours a month
2. Tell what was easy/difficult
3. Reflect on how you see keyboarding affecting other classes, other assignments, life in general

February-May

Spend 15 minutes, four times a week, for the entire month, on Type to Learn (or another typing program from appendix—NOT DanceMat Typing). If you use TTL, the teacher can track progress.

Go through lessons progressively keeping eyes on text. Practice hitting the return key without looking. DON'T CORRECT MISTAKES! You are trying to learn the keys, not how to fix mistakes. If you are practicing at home regularly, you will see a big difference in typing speed and accuracy.

The third week, cover keys with a light cloth so you cannot see your hands. Do all exercises for the rest of the month with hands covered. The goal: to memorize location of keys without taking your eyes from the screen and improve speed and accuracy.

On last day of month, submit your homework via dropbox (or email if dropbox not available). Write 3-5 sentences addressing on the following:

- Verify you have completed homework. That is, you typed 15 minutes 4 times a week (for one hour a week) for four weeks, for a total of four hours a month
- Tell what was easy/difficult
- Reflect on how you see keyboarding affecting other classes, other assignments, life in general

Fourth Grade Keyboarding

FOURTH GRADE

OVERVIEW

Reinforce basics of key position, posture and hand position. Continue accuracy and technique. Set grade level goal of 25wpm—fast enough to keep up with 4th grade demands and faster than most students can handwrite

Objectives and Steps

_____Keyboarding is a cumulative skill. What can be effectively learned in one grade depends heavily upon what is learned in earlier years. If hunt 'n peck habits become ingrained, it's difficult to develop keyboarding competence in later years.

_____During the first keyboard class of the year, tour the keyboard. Review:

- *Backspace and delete—what's the difference between these?*
- *Tab—what's this used for?*
- *Home row, QWERTY row, lower row*
- *Numeric keypad—works for numbers if NumLock invoked*
- *Ctrl, Alt keys—share some uses of these two keys*

_____Basics to remember during fourth grade are:

- *Keep hands on home row*
- *Use correct posture for all typing (keyboard practice and practical applications)*
    - *Sit straight, shoulders back, head up, body centered in front of keyboard, feet flat on ground*
    - *Keep elbows close to sides*
    - *Have fingers slightly curved*
    - *Use thumb for spacebar*
    - *Place keyboard one inch from edge of table*

- *Focus on touch typing*
- *Keep copy to the side of keyboard, eyes on copy or screen—NOT keyboard*
- *Key with a steady even pace*
- *Use keyboard shortcuts (i.e., Ctrl+B, Shift+Alt+D)*
- *Apply keyboard skills whenever possible, not just during typing practice*

____Fourth grade focus is touch typing, which requires the memorization of keys. Once students know key placement, speed and accuracy will come (don't worry if it doesn't happen until 5-8th grade. That's common).

____Start **Month #1** with five minutes of finger warm-ups. Repeat several times a month. These show students that they have ten working fingers. Go to (http://learnkeyboarding.wikispaces.com/Keyboarding+Warm-ups) for fun exercises fourth graders love.

____Work on one keyboard row at a time, one per month, using Dance Mat Typing and Nimble Fingers. Yes, you remember they did this in third grade. It takes repetition to memorize key placement. Here's a schedule for **Months #1, #2, and #3**:

- *first month: home row*
- *second month: QWERTY row*
- *third month: lower row*

Best Practices

- *Students should type as fast as they need to for classwork. Set a goal of 25wpm—exceeding the speed most students can handwrite.*
- *Focus on speed and accuracy while remembering good habits like proper hand and body position.*
- *Work on age-appropriate keyboard shortkeys*
- *Cover keys when practicing*

____Students practice 10-15 minutes during class time and 45 minutes per week as homework on this schedule of one row per month (see homework at end of Third Grade Unit).

____During the first keyboarding session of the year, walk around and check key posture points (see above).

____Typing is best learned in projects that collaborate with classroom learning and require the use of keyboarding. No later than **Month #2**, begin a series of project-based typing using MS Word or Publisher (or similar). These will provide a framework for learning keyboarding as students integrate it into classroom inquiry. These can be short reports, magazines, trifolds, a story—pick one that works for your school environment. Reinforce use of enter key to end paragraphs, word-wrap to go to next line, tab to indent, and the purpose of cursor in word processing. See end of this unit for project examples (courtesy Structured Learning Fourth Grade Technology Curriculum).

_____**Each grading period**, students take a blank keyboard quiz (see end of unit for example) to test knowledge of key placement. Give them about fifteen minutes. They can work in pairs and must retake until they pass. This works—I often see students memorizing key placement so they can pass the next time. This knowledge quickly translates to improved speed and accuracy.

_____**Each grading period,** students take a keyboard quiz to determine speed and accuracy (see sample under Third Grade unit. Or, use a few pages from a book students are reading.) As students type, anecdotally notice who is using all fingers and has correct posture. Those that aren't, lose points.

_____After the quiz, allow one minute to correct spelling errors by right-clicking on the red squiggly lines (discuss green and blue squiggles, but skip them. My experience is they are as likely to be wrong as right).

_____The first quiz of the year is the benchmark. The rest are graded based on improvement:

- *20% improvement* — *10/10*
- *10-20% improvement* — *9/10*
- *1-10% improvement* — *8/10*
- *No improvement* — *7/10*
- *Slowed down* — *6/10*

_____Grade level standards are:

3rd Grade: 15 wpm	*6th Grade: 35 wpm*
4th Grade: 25 wpm	*7th Grade: 40 wpm*
5th Grade: 30 wpm	*8th Grade: 45 wpm*

_____Post a list of 'keyboard speedsters' on the bulletin board—students who reached grade level standard. You may decide to give awards—something that works for your school. In my classes, students get a free dress pass (we are a uniform school).

_____**Month #4** (following completion of study of all three keyboard rows), students switch to Type to Learn (installed software) or Typing Web (online—free) for class practice and homework. By this time, students should have all keys memorized so students cover their hands with a cloth any time they are practicing keyboard drills (not during projects requiring keyboarding). They'll be surprised at first that it's so much more difficult when they can't see their fingers. They'll argue that they know where the keys are, just not with their hands covered, and they'll finally capitulate—especially when they see classmates doing fine.

_____**Consistently throughout the year**, introduce and reinforce the use of keyboard shortcuts such as these:

- *When logging in, expect students to independently strike Ctr+Alt+Del and type in user name and password*
- *When unable to exit a program, expect students to try Alt+F4 before requesting assistance*
- *When saving, have students Ctrl+S*
- *When printing, have students Ctrl+P*
- *When needing to undo an action, remind students to try Ctrl+Z before giving in to frustration*
- *When copying something, Ctrl+C*
- *When pasting something, Ctrl+V (Ask students why not Ctrl+P?)*
- *When enlarging a window, double click*
- *When toggling between two windows (say, for research), Alt+Tab*
- *When entering date, Shift+Alt+D*
- *When exiting a program, Alt+F4*

Students love to show off their techie-ness with these.

_____Somewhere around **Month #6**, test students to determine who can type faster than they handwrite. Do this by circling back on science class and the scientific method:

- Do students remember this experiment from last year? What were the results? Remind them—last year, most students handwrote faster than they could type.
- Discuss whether students think this has changed. Ask students to share thoughts on how they reached their conclusion. You are likely to get opinions on both sides of this discussion. If not, prod students with logic for both.
- Suggest running an experiment similar to last year's to see which is faster for fourth graders—handwriting or typing.
- Discuss the Scientific Method, its various steps, its applicability to general problem solving (such as this issue), and then

develop a hypothesis for keyboarding vs. handwriting, maybe: *Fourth grade students in Mr. Q's class can handwrite faster than they type*.

- Have them hand-copy the typing quiz they took earlier in the trimester for 3 minutes.
- Analyze the results: Compare their handwriting speed to typing speed.
- Discuss results: Why do students think some students type faster and others slower? (In my classes, fourth graders typed about as fast as they handwrote—approx. 18wpm—although a good-sized group typed close to 25 wpm—the class requirement. Discussion was heated and enthusiastic on reasons. Especially valuable were the thoughts of those who typed faster).
- Students will offer lots of reasons for slower typing (they're new to typing, don't do it much in class, they got distracted). One noteworthy reason is that students don't usually type from copy (quite valid, I think—don't you?). Key in on this reason and revise the experiment to have students type and handwrite from a prompt.
- Give students a prompt and one minute to collect their thoughts. Remind them how they construct a five-paragraph essay (or use your school's writing guidelines)—1) introduction, 2-4) one paragraph per point, 5) conclusion. Take their one minute to think through the prompt with these guidelines in mind.
- What is the conclusion? Analyze these results.
- If possible, share results from 5-8th. What grade level do students consistently type faster than they handwrite? Why? Are students surprised by the answer? If appropriate, ask if students think social networks like Facebook and Twitter have an impact on typing speed.
- Post a list on the wall of students who type faster than they handwrite. This surprises everyone.
- Note: There is lots of variance in the steps of the scientific method when talking about elementary grades. Talk to your science teacher and adapt this experiment to the ones s/he uses.

_____**Occasionally throughout the year**, have students use a program called TypingTest.com to see how their speed and accuracy is progressing. This is a fun site, one which students will have fun visiting during free time.

_____Keep keyboarding fun, but help students develop good habits. They'll need these as speed and accuracy become more important.

_____A typical keyboarding lesson for 4th grade looks like this:

- Devote 10-15 minutes of each 45-minute session to keyboarding practice, reviewing homework that's due and coming up. Leave the rest to supporting classroom units of inquiry with projects that require typing (as noted earlier in this lesson)
- Mix up the 10-15 minutes with the following:
  - Keyboard practice
  - Online keyboarding websites
  - Finger practice
  - Keyboard quizzes
- Throughout classes, remind students of shortkeys that accomplish oft-repeated activities like copy, paste, print, save, undo.

_____**Extension**: At the end of the year, have a Team Challenge. Click here for example (scroll to Week 3) or go to the end of the Third Grade unit for questions I use. Break the class into teams. Ask a question from the list and give only three seconds to answer. They can answer verbally or with the correct finger. The focus is on speed—students must know the answers, not have to think about it.

_____**Trouble shooting**: I can't type with hands covered. *Keep practicing.*

Need help? Go to http://askatechteacher.com

SCOPE AND SEQUENCE CHECKLIST

Problem-solving

_____*Volume doesn't work—check plugs*
_____*Monitor doesn't work—check power*
_____*Keyboard doesn't work—check plugs, reboot*
_____*Computer doesn't work—check power*
_____*Difference between save and save-as*
_____*Learn fifteen basic keyboard shortcuts (Alt+F4, Esc, Ctrl+P, Ctrl+S, Ctrl+C, Ctrl+V, Ctrl+Alt+Del, double-click to enlarge window, Alt+Tab, ???)*
Can't close a program—Alt+F4

Posture

_____*Keyboard one inch off edge of table*
_____*Correct posture—legs in front, body in front, elbows at sides*
_____*Keep feet flat on the floor, body one hand's width from table*
_____*Sit straight, body centered*
_____*Hands curled over homerow (not flat)*
_____*Fingers rest on home row keys*

Keyboarding

_____*Use proper log-on/log-off procedures.*
_____*Use proper care and handling of keyboard*
_____*Learn difference between backspace, delete*
_____*Understand all keyboard keys*
_____*Use lab software for keyboarding*
_____*Use internet-based sites for keyboarding*
_____*Keyboard goal of 25 wpm*
_____*Can touch type all letter keys*
_____*Can compose at keyboard*
_____*When typing, fingers move—not hands*
_____*Adopt a reach with fingers—which keeps hands on home row*
_____*In general, use outside fingers for outside keys, inside fingers for inside keys*
_____*Compose at keyboard with ease*

FOURTH GRADE TYPING PROJECTS

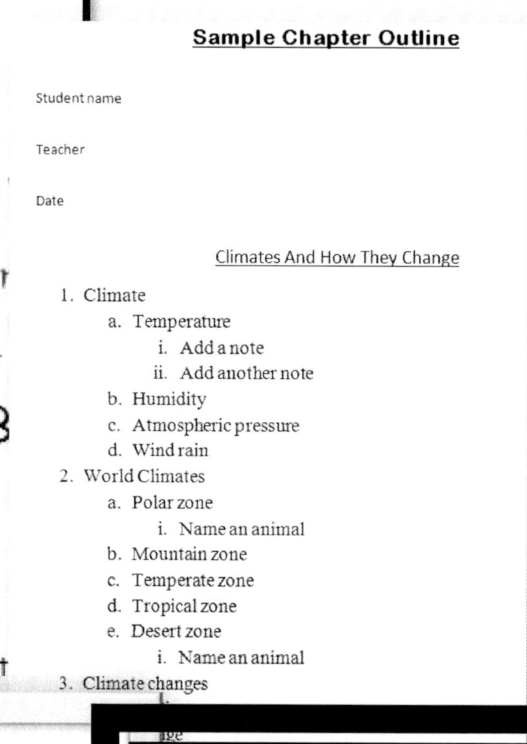

FOURTH GRADE BLANK KEYBOARD QUIZ

These keyboarding hints come directly from the classroom, tested on over 400 students a year. These are the most common fixes that help students excel at keyboarding

1. Tuck elbows against sides of your body. This keeps hands in the right spot—home row
2. Use your thumb for the space bar. That leaves hands on home row
3. Curl fingers over home row—they're cat paws, not dog paws
4. Use inside fingers for inside keys, outside fingers for outside keys
5. Use the finger closest to the key you need. Sounds simple, but this isn't what usually happens with beginners.
6. Keep pointers anchored to f and j
7. Play keyboard like a piano (or violin, or guitar, or recorder). You'd never use your pointer for all keys
8. Fingers move, not your hands. Hands stay anchored to the f and j keys
9. Don't use caps lock for capitals! Use shift.
10. Add a barrier between sides of the keyboards. I fashioned one from cover stock. That'll remind students to stay on the correct side of keyboard

Fifth Grade Keyboarding

FIFTH GRADE

OVERVIEW

Reinforce key position, posture and hand position. Continue with accuracy and technique. Begin work on speed with grade level goal of 30 wpm

Objectives and Steps

_____Keyboarding is a cumulative skill. What can be effectively learned in one grade depends heavily upon what is learned in earlier years. If hunt 'n peck habits become ingrained, it's difficult to develop keyboarding competence in later years.

_____During the first keyboard class of the year, tour the keyboard. Review:

- *Backspace and delete—what's the difference between these?*
- *Tab—what's this used for?*
- *F row—what are these used for?*
- *Windows key—what's a use of it?*
- *Right-mouse key—who knows where that is?*
- *What's the tilde for?*
- *What are the bracket keys for?*
- *Home row, QWERTY row, lower row*
- *Numeric keypad—works for numbers if NumLock invoked*
- *Ctrl, Alt keys—what are some shortkeys that include these*

_____Basics to remember during fifth grade are:

- *Keep hands on home row*
- *Use correct posture and keyboarding skills for all typing (keyboard practice and practical applications)*

- *Sit straight, shoulders back, head up, body centered in front of keyboard and one hands-width from table, feet flat on ground*
- *Keep elbows close to sides*
- *Have fingers slightly curved*
- *Use thumb for spacebar*
- *Place keyboard one inch from edge of table*

- *Focus on touch typing*
- *Keep copy to the side of keyboard, eyes on copy or screen—NOT keyboard*
- *Key with a steady even pace*
- *Use keyboard shortcuts (i.e., Ctrl+B, Shift+Alt+D)*

> **Best Practices**
>
> - *Students should learn to type as fast as they need to for classwork. Set a goal of 30wpm—exceeding the speed most students handwrite*
> - *Focus on speed and accuracy while using good keyboarding habits*
> - *Use shortkeys wherever possible*
> - *Cover keys when practicing*

_____Fifth grade focus is touch typing, which requires memorizing keys. Once students know key placement, speed and accuracy will come (don't worry if it doesn't happen this year. Keep working at it. It'll come).

_____Start **Month #1** with five minutes of finger warm-ups, Repeat these several times a month to show students that they have eight fingers (and one thumb—don't use left thumb) that work. Go to (http://learnkeyboarding.wikispaces.com/Keyboarding+Warm-ups) for fun exercises fifth graders love.

_____As in fourth grade, work on one keyboard row at a time, one per month, using Dance Mat Typing and Nimble Fingers. Yes, you remember they did this in fourth grade (and third grade). It takes repetition to memorize key placement. Here's a schedule for **Months #1, #2, and #3**:

- *first month: home row*
- *second month: QWERTY row*
- *third month: lower row*

_____Students practice 10-15 minutes during class time and 45 minutes per week as homework on this schedule of one row per month (see homework at end of Third Grade Unit).

_____During the first keyboarding session of the year, walk around and check to be sure all key posture points are followed (see above).

_____Typing is best learned in projects that collaborate with classroom learning and require the use of keyboarding. No later than **Month #2**, begin project-based typing using MS Word or Publisher (or similar) that integrates into classroom units. These can be short reports, magazines, trifolds, a story—pick one that works for your school environment. Reinforce use of enter key to end paragraphs, word-wrap to go to next line, tab to indent, cursor placement to insert objects. See the end of this unit for examples (courtesy of the Structured Learning Fifth Grade Technology Curriculum).

_____**Each grading period**, students take a blank keyboard quiz (see end of Fourth Grade unit for example) to test knowledge of key placement. Give them ten-fifteen minutes. They can work in pairs and must retake until they pass. This works—I often see students memorizing key placement so they can pass the next time. This knowledge quickly translates to improved speed and accuracy.

_____**Each grading period,** students take a keyboard quiz to determine speed and accuracy (see sample under Third Grade unit. Or, use a few pages from a book students are reading.) As students take this quiz, anecdotally notice who is using all fingers and correct posture. Those that aren't, lose points.

_____After the quiz, allow one minute to correct spelling errors by right-clicking on the red squiggly lines (discuss green and blue squiggles, but skip them. My experience is they are as likely to be wrong as right).

_____The first quiz of the year is the benchmark. The rest are graded based on improvement:

- *20% improvement* *10/10*
- *10-20% improvement* *9/10*
- *1-10% improvement* *8/10*
- *No improvement* *7/10*
- *Slowed down* *6/10*

_____Grade level standards are:

5th Grade: 30 wpm *7th Grade: 40 wpm*
6th Grade: 35wpm *8th Grade: 45 wpm*

_____Post a list of students who reached the grade level standard. You may decide to give them an award—something that works for your school. In my classes, students get a free dress pass (we are a uniform school), which is quite exciting for them.

_____**Month #4,** after finishing a month on each of three rows, have students practice the simplest form of touch typing by mastering two-letter words (http://www.nimblefingers.com/teachers.htm#checkit—scroll to bottom).

This will be difficult at first, and then fun—like a game. Help them stick with it through impossible to challenging to huzzah.

_____**Month #5**, students switch to Type to Learn (installed software) or Typing Web (online—free) for class-time practice and homework. Students should have all keys memorized so cover their hands with a cloth any time they are practicing keyboarding (not during projects requiring keyboarding). They'll be surprised at first that it's so much more difficult when they can't see their fingers. They'll argue that they know where the keys are, just not with their hands covered, and they'll finally capitulate when they see classmates doing fine.

_____**Consistently throughout the year**, reinforce the use of keyboard shortcuts (see a list under the Third Grade unit). These are quick macros that accomplish commonly-performed tasks. For example:

- *When unable to exit a program, expect students to try Alt+F4 before requesting assistance*
- *When saving, have students Ctrl+S*
- *When printing, have students Ctrl+P*
- *When needing to undo an action, students Ctrl+Z before giving in to frustration*
- *When copying something, Ctrl+C*
- *When pasting something, Ctrl+V (why not Ctrl+P?)*
- *When enlarging a window, double click the title bar*
- *When unable to close a program, Alt+F4*
- *When toggling between two windows (say, for research), Alt+Tab*
- *When entering date, Shift+Alt+D*
- *When the taskbar disappears (some pesky student hid it), push the Windows key*
- *When indenting in a list, use Tab and Shift+Tab*

Students love to show off their techie-ness with these.

_____Somewhere around **Month #6**, test students to determine who can type faster than they can handwrite. Do this by circling back on science class and the scientific method:

- Do students remember this experiment from last year? What were the results? Remind them—last year, students were evenly split—some typed faster, some handwrote faster (or, whatever your results were).
- Discuss whether students think this has changed. Ask students to share thoughts on how they reached their conclusion. You are

likely to get opinions on both sides of this discussion. If not, prod students with logic for both.

- Suggest running an experiment similar to last year's to see which is faster for fifth graders—handwriting or typing.
- Discuss the Scientific Method, its various steps, its applicability to general problem solving (such as this issue), and then develop a hypothesis for keyboarding vs. handwriting, maybe: *Fifth grade students in Ms. K's class can handwrite faster than they type*.
- Have them hand-copy the typing quiz they took earlier in the trimester for 3 minutes.
- Analyze the results: Compare their handwriting speed to typing speed.
- Discuss results: Why do students think some students type faster and others slower? (In my classes, fifth graders consistently typed faster than they handwrote—approx. 20 wpm vs. 24 wpm. Discussion was heated and enthusiastic on reasons).
- Students will offer lots of reasons for slower typing, but key in on one that suggests students don't usually type from copy (quite valid, don't you think?).
- Give students a prompt and one minute to collect their thoughts. Remind them how they construct a five-paragraph essay (or use your school's writing guidelines)—1) introduction, 2-4) one paragraph per point, 5) conclusion. Take one minute to think through the prompt with these guidelines in mind.
- What is the conclusion? Analyze results.
- Post a list on the wall of students who type faster than they handwrite.
- Note: There is lots of variance in the steps of the scientific method when talking about elementary grades. Talk to your science teacher and adapt this experiment to the ones s/he uses.

____**Occasionally through the year**, have students use a program called TypingTest.com to see how their speed and accuracy is progressing. This is a fun site, one which you can encourage students to visit on their own.

____**Sometime during the year**, introduce students to ASCII art. ASCII art is that amazing computer drawing where keyboard letters become a picture (see inset). Done well, it never fails to impress friends with the student's consummate keyboarding skills.

____Here's a simple way to do this that every student can accomplish:

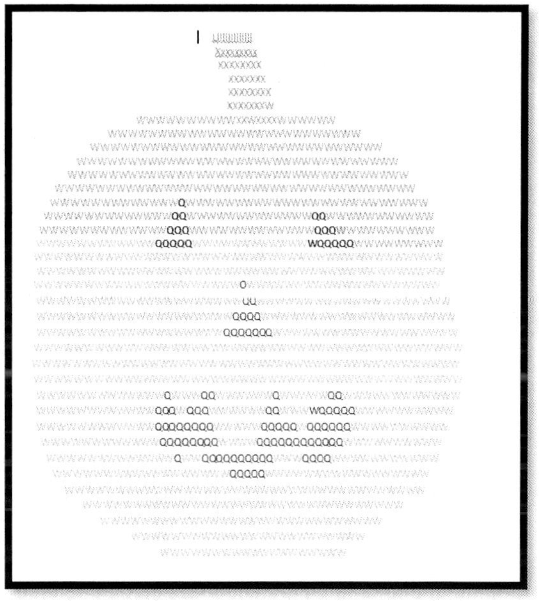

- *Add a watermark of a picture you like to MS Word or another word processing program. A single image works best—one without a complicated background.*
- *Type over it with appropriate letters (if you're more patient than I, you can pick a variety of letters, numbers and symbols to provide more depth)*
- *Highlight the appropriate letters/symbols and change the color to fit the image*
- *Delete the watermark from the page. Now all that's left is the letters/numbers/symbols you type.*
- *How long did the inset take me? About twenty minutes.*

_____It can be simple as seen in the inset or more sophisticated (see sample under Fifth Grade Typing Projects at end of this lesson). The first takes about one class. The second takes as long as the student wants.

_____This ASCII art can support a classroom unit of inquiry, in place of any spot students would use a picture.

_____Another example you'll see on the Fifth Grade Typing Projects page is a Tagxedo. Click the link (or Google 'Tagxedo') and follow the directions to create an image out of words and phrases.

_____Use any project that keeps keyboarding fun while developing good habits.

_____A typical keyboarding lesson for 5th grade looks like this:

- Devote 10-15 minutes of each 45-minute session to keyboarding practice, reviewing homework that's due and coming up. Leave the rest to supporting classroom units of inquiry with projects that require typing
- Mix up the 10-15 minutes with the following:
  - *Keyboarding software practice*
  - *Online keyboarding websites*
  - *Finger practice*
  - *Typing Tests*

- Throughout all lessons, remind students of shortkeys that can accomplish oft-repeated activities like copy, paste, print, save, undo.

____**Extension**: At the end of the year, have a Team Challenge. Click here for example (scroll to Week 3) or go to the end of the Third Grade unit for questions I use. Break the class into teams. Ask a question from the list and give only three seconds to answer. They can answer verbally or with the correct finger. The focus is on speed—students must know the answers, not have to think about it.

____**Trouble shooting**: I can't type with hands covered. *Keep practicing.*

Need help? Go to http://askatechteacher.com

Notes

____

____

____

____

____

____

____

____.

SCOPE AND SEQUENCE

Problem-solving

_____*Double click doesn't work—push enter*
_____*Volume doesn't work—check plugs*
_____*Monitor doesn't work—check power*
_____*Keyboard doesn't work—check plugs, reboot*
_____*Computer doesn't work—check power*
_____*Difference between save and save-as*
_____*Browser doesn't work—try a different browser*

Posture

_____*Keyboard one inch off edge of table*
_____*Correct posture—legs in front, body in front, elbows at sides*
_____*Keep feet flat on the floor*
_____*Sit straight, body centered one hand's width from table*
_____*Hands curled over homerow (not flat)*
_____*Copy to the side of keyboard*

Keyboarding

_____*Use proper log-on/log-off procedures.*
_____*Demonstrate proper care and handling of keyboard*
_____*Understand difference between backspace, delete*
_____*Understand all keyboard keys*
_____*Rest fingers on home row keys, reach for other keys*
_____*Learn twenty basic keyboard shortcuts (Alt+F4, Esc, Ctrl+P, Ctrl+S, Ctrl+C, Ctrl+V, Ctrl+Alt+Del, double-click to enlarge window, Alt+Tab, Win key, Shift+Tab, right mouse button key, ???)*
_____*Use lab software for keyboarding*
_____*Use internet-based sites for keyboarding*
_____*Key paragraphs with enter and tab*
_____*Set keyboard goal at 30 wpm*
_____*Touch type all keys*
_____*Keep eyes on copy most of the time*
_____*Touch type many two- and three- letter words and phrases with speed and accuracy*
_____*Compose at keyboard with ease*

FIFTH GRADE TYPING PROJECTS

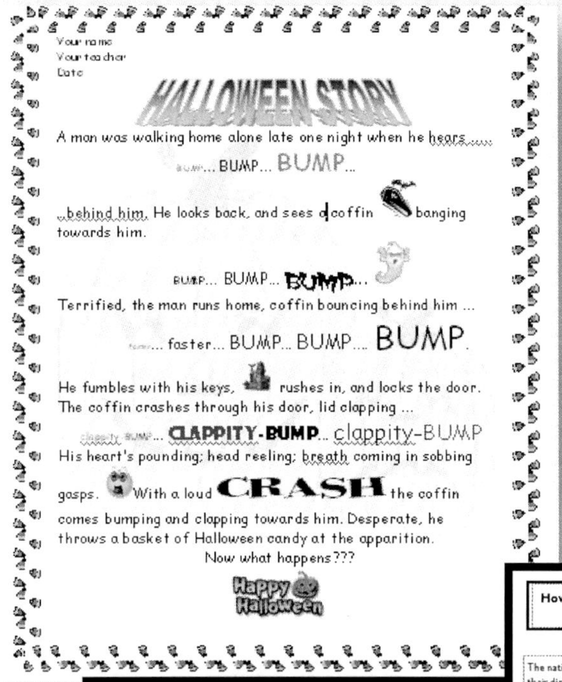
Your name
Your teacher
Date

HALLOWEEN STORY

A man was walking home alone late one night when he hears......

bump... BUMP... BUMP...

...behind him. He looks back, and sees a coffin banging towards him.

bump... BUMP... BUMP...

Terrified, the man runs home, coffin bouncing behind him ...

faster... faster... BUMP... BUMP... BUMP.

He fumbles with his keys, rushes in, and locks the door. The coffin crashes through his door, lid clapping ...

clappity bump... CLAPPITY-BUMP... clappity-BUMP

His heart's pounding; head reeling; breath coming in sobbing gasps. With a loud CRASH the coffin comes bumping and clapping towards him. Desperate, he throws a basket of Halloween candy at the apparition.

Now what happens???

Happy Halloween

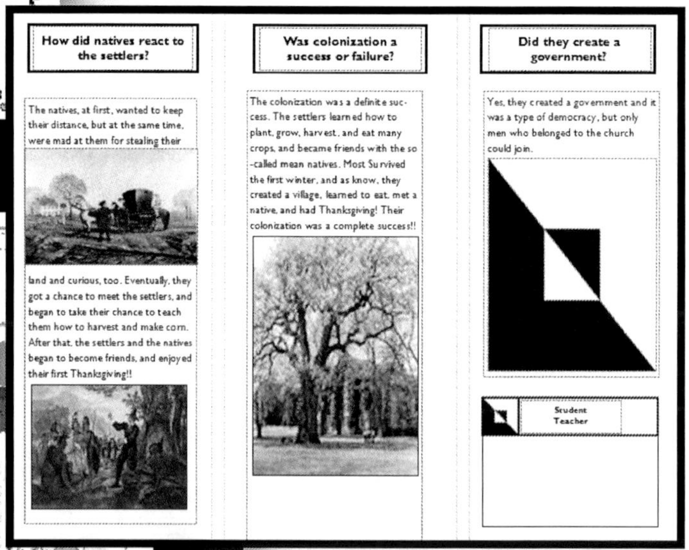
How did natives react to the settlers?

The natives, at first, wanted to keep their distance, but at the same time, were mad at them for stealing their land and curious, too. Eventually, they got a chance to meet the settlers, and began to take their chance to teach them how to harvest and make corn. After that, the settlers and the natives began to become friends, and enjoyed their first Thanksgiving!!

Was colonization a success or failure?

The colonization was a definite success. The settlers learned how to plant, grow, harvest, and eat many crops, and became friends with the so-called mean natives. Most Survived the first winter, and as know, they created a village, learned to eat, met a native, and had Thanksgiving! Their colonization was a complete success!!

Did they create a government?

Yes, they created a government and it was a type of democracy, but only men who belonged to the church could join.

Student
Teacher

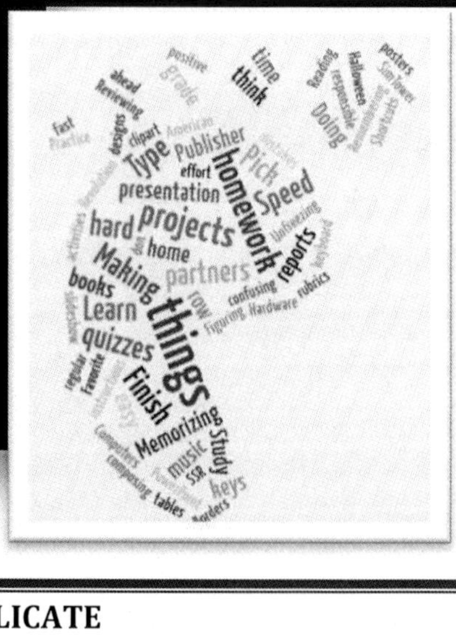

Sixth –Eighth Grade Keyboarding

SIXTH-EIGHTH GRADE

OVERVIEW

Work on all essential elements of keyboarding—technique, speed, and accuracy—with grade level goal of 35-45 wpm

Objectives and Steps

_____Keyboarding is a cumulative skill. What can be effectively learned in one grade depends heavily upon what is learned in earlier years. If hunt 'n peck habits become ingrained, it's difficult to develop keyboarding competence in later years.

_____Basics to remember in sixth-eighth grade are:

- *Keep hands on home row*
- *Use correct posture and keyboarding skills for all typing (keyboard practice and practical applications)*
    - *Sit straight, shoulders back, head up, body centered in front of keyboard about one hand's width from table, feet flat on ground*
    - *Keep elbows close to sides*
    - *Have fingers slightly curved over home row*
    - *Reach for keys—don't move hands (only fingers move)*
- *Focus on touch typing*
- *Keep copy to the side of keyboard, eyes on copy or screen—NOT keyboard*
- *Key with a steady even pace*
- *Use keyboard shortcuts (i.e., Ctrl+B, Shift+Alt+D)*

_____Sixth grade is a combination of the following typing activities:

- *Key memorization with:*
    - *Work on each row*
    - *Work on two-letter words and common phrases*
    - *One-time Brown Bear typing challenge*
- *Continuous practice with a graduated keyboarding program like Type to Learn or Typing Web*
- *Covered hands during all typing practice. They will want to memorize key placement so this is easier.*
- *Continuous reinforcement of shortkeys to remind students that keyboarding makes typing faster, easier and more fun*
- *Anecdotal observation by teacher of typing skills—posture, hand position, finger use, etc.*
- *Monthly finger warm-ups as a reminder that all fingers are used for keyboarding and all of them function*
- *Quarterly quizzes*
- *Yearly (or bi-yearly) keyboard challenge to test student ability to remember skills associated with touch typing (see notes under fourth grade keyboarding lesson)*

> ## *Best Practices*
>
> - *Students learn to type as fast as they need to for classwork. Set a goal of 35-45 wpm—exceeding the speed students handwrite.*
> - *Focus on speed and accuracy, but remember good habits like proper hand and body position.*
> - *Work on age-appropriate keyboard shortkeys*
> - *Cover keys when practicing*

____Start **Month #1** with five minutes of finger warm-ups, Repeat these once a month to show students that they have ten fingers that work. Go to (http://learnkeyboarding.wikispaces.com/Keyboarding+Warm-ups) for fun exercises middle schoolers love.

____As in fifth grade, **start the year** by working on one keyboard row at a time, using Dance Mat Typing, Typing Lessons, Peter's Online Typing Course, or Nimble Fingers. Students practice during class time (fifteen minutes a week) and at home (three sessions of fifteen minutes each, every week).

____Here's a schedule for the **first six weeks**:

- *Weeks 1-2: home row*
- *Weeks 3-4: QWERTY row*
- *Weeks 5-6: lower row*

_____Students practice 10-15 minutes during class and 45 minutes per week as homework on this schedule.

_____During the **first keyboarding session of the year**, walk around and check to be sure all key posture points are followed (see above).

_____**By Month #3** (after two weeks on each of three rows), have students practice the simplest form of touch typing by mastering two-letter words (http://www.nimblefingers.com/teachers.htm#checkit—scroll to bottom). This will be difficult at first, and then fun—like a game. Help them stick with it through impossible to challenging to huzzah.

_____Have students take a fun 'test' before moving on to the graduated typing program they will spend the balance of the year on. Remember Brown Bear Typing—a favorite from kindergarten, first and second grades? Return to it and have a fifteen-minute contest to see who can get the highest score. This focuses solely on key placement—no worries about hand positions. Award the winner something that suits your student group.

_____**Month #4,** students switch to Type to Learn (installed purchased software) or Typing Web (online—free). This is where they'll spend the rest of their typing practice time for the year. Students must cover hands while practicing. I provide cloths they use at school and take home if they'd like. It feels hard at first and quickly becomes easier. The focus is on speed and accuracy.

_____As students type, anecdotally observe posture, hand position, eye placement. Make suggestions to the class when you see an endemic problem.

_____Typing is best learned in projects that collaborate with classroom learning and require the use of keyboarding. No later than **Month #2**, begin project-based typing using MS Word or Publisher (or similar) that integrates into classroom units. These can be short reports, magazines, trifolds, a story—pick one that works for your school environment. Reinforce use of enter key to end paragraphs, word-wrap to go to next line, tab to indent, and purpose of cursor in word processing.

_____**Each grading period**, students take a ten-fifteen minute blank keyboard quiz (see end of Fourth Grade unit for example) to test knowledge of key placement. They can work in pairs and must retake until they pass. This knowledge quickly translates to speed and accuracy.

_____**Each grading period,** students take a keyboard quiz using TypingTest.com to determine speed and accuracy. Take a three-minute warm-up and then the three-minute test. As students take this quiz, anecdotally notice who is using all fingers and correct posture. Those that aren't, lose points.

_____The first quiz of the year is the benchmark. The rest are graded based on improvement:

- *20% improvement* *10/10*
- *10-20% improvement* *9/10*
- *1-10% improvement* *8/10*
- *No improvement* *7/10*
- *Slowed down* *6/10*

_____Grade level standards are:

5th Grade: 30 wpm	*7th Grade: 40 wpm*
6th Grade: 35wpm	*8th Grade: 45 wpm*

_____Observe students as they type and evaluate their errors. The cause of the error is often more important than the fact that the student made a mistake. Many errors are symptoms of faulty keyboarding technique, wrong finger curve, eyes not on copy, or posture.

- Errors such as reversals, typing an "e" instead of an "r", and omission or addition of letters are more often due to poor planning or thinking than they are to inaccurate finger placement.
- Other causes of errors include tension, wandering attention, faulty reading, or the wrong mind set.
- Watch students for signs of fatigue, moving heads, massaging, or tight facial expressions.

_____**Consistently throughout the year**, reinforce the use of keyboard shortcuts (see a list under the Third Grade unit). These are quick macros that accomplish commonly-performed tasks. For example:

- *When unable to exit a program, expect students to try Alt+F4 before requesting assistance*
- *When saving, have students Ctrl+S*
- *When printing, have students Ctrl+P*
- *When needing to undo an action, students Ctrl+Z before giving in to frustration*
- *When copying something, Ctrl+C*
- *When pasting something, Ctrl+V (why not Ctrl+P?)*
- *When enlarging a window, double click the title bar*
- *When unable to close a program, Alt+F4*
- *When toggling between two windows (say, for research), Alt+Tab*

- *When entering date, Shift+Alt+D*
- *When the taskbar disappears (some pesky student hid it), push the Windows key*
- *When indenting in a list, use Tab and Shift+Tab*

Students love to show off their techie-ness with these.

_____A typical keyboarding lesson for 6th-8th grade looks like this:

- Devote 10-15 minutes of each 45-minute session to keyboarding practice, reviewing homework that's due and coming up. Leave the rest to supporting classroom units of inquiry with projects that require typing.
- Mix up the 10-15 minutes with the following:
    - *Keyboarding software practice*
    - *Online keyboarding websites*
    - *Finger practice*
    - *Typing Tests*
- Throughout lessons, remind students of shortkeys that accomplish oft-repeated activities like copy, paste, print, save, undo.

_____**Extension**: At the end of the year, have a Team Challenge. Click here for example (scroll to Week 3) or go to the end of the Third Grade unit for questions I use. Break the class into teams. Ask a question from the list and give only three seconds to answer. They can answer verbally or with the correct finger. The focus is on speed—students must know the answers, not have to think about it.

_____**Trouble shooting**: I can't type with hands covered. *Keep practicing.*

Need help? Go to http://askatechteacher.com

Notes

____

____

____

_________________________.

SCOPE AND SEQUENCE CHECKLIST

Problem-solving

- _____*Volume doesn't work—check plugs*
- _____*Monitor doesn't work—check power*
- _____*Keyboard doesn't work—check plugs, reboot*
- _____*Computer doesn't work—check power*
- _____*Difference between save and save-as*
- _____*Browser doesn't work—try a different browser*

Posture

- _____*Keyboard one inch off edge of table*
- _____*Correct posture—legs in front, body in front, elbows at sides*
- _____*Keep feet flat on the floor*
- _____*Sit straight, body centered one hand's width from table*
- _____*Hands curled over homerow (not flat)*
- _____*Copy to the side of keyboard*

Keyboarding

- _____*Demonstrate proper care and handling of keyboard*
- _____*Understand difference between backspace, delete*
- _____*Understand all keyboard keys*
- _____*Understand use of arrow keys*
- _____*Rest fingers on home row, reach for other keys. When viewed, hands should appear still with fingers moving—no flying hands.*
- _____*Learn twenty basic keyboard shortcuts (Alt+F4, Esc, Ctrl+P, Ctrl+S, Ctrl+C, Ctrl+V, Ctrl+Alt+Del, Ctrl+B/I/U, double-click to enlarge window, Alt+Tab, Win key, Shift+Tab, right mouse button key, Ctrl+ (to zoom in), Ctrl- (to zoom out), ???)*
- _____*Use lab software for keyboarding*
- _____*Use internet-based sites for keyboarding*
- _____*Key paragraphs with enter and tab*
- _____*Set keyboard goal at 30 wpm*
- _____*Touch type all keys*
- _____*Keep eyes on copy most of the time*
- _____*Touch type many two- and three- letter words and phrases with speed and accuracy*
- _____*Compose at keyboard with ease*

More Online Typing Practice (and Games)

(Click here or visit ***http://askatechteacher.wordpress.com/great-websites-for-kids/keyboarding-websites/*** *for online list)*

1. Alpha Attack Typing Game
2. Dance Mat Typing
3. Finger jig practice game
4. Free Typing Games
5. Free Typing Test
6. Free typing tutor
7. Keyboard challenge—grade level
8. Keyboard practice—quick start
9. Keyboard test—quick, adjustable
10. Keyboard—free online typing course
11. Keyboarding for Kids
12. Keyboarding resources listed
13. Keyboarding—full online course
14. Keyboarding—games
15. Keyboarding—lessons
16. Keyboarding—lessons and speed quiz
17. Keyboarding—more lessons
18. Keyboarding—quick start
19. Keyboarding—speed quiz
20. Mrkent.com
21. NitroTyping
22. NitroTyping
23. Online practice—quick start
24. Online typing course
25. Online typing lessons
26. Online typing lessons — even more
27. Online typing lessons — more
28. Power Typing
29. Power Typing Tutor
30. Sense-Lang- Typing Games
31. Touch Typing Progressive Program
32. Type Online
33. Typing Defense—fun word practice
34. Typing Drills
35. Typing Master Games
36. Typing program—a graduated course
37. Typing Test

What About Those Lefties?

Dear Otto is an occasional column on my blog where I answer questions I get from readers about teaching tech. Here's a great question I got from Sandy:

Q: I am a Computer Teacher for Early Education (3 & 4 year olds) and also Elementary-age students. My question to you is if a child is left handed, should you teach them to use their mouse with their left hand?

A: I've seen lots of different answers, but there's only one that makes sense to me: Allow students to use the hand they're most comfortable with. If they want to use the left, I set the mouse up so it works for them. Often, it's a shared station, so I help the (older) student get used to reversing the mouse buttons themselves (Youngers: just move the mouse). They may decide using the right hand is simpler, but older students may be eager to visit the control panel and set the mouse up to suit their needs. You may want to set up one class computer as a 'lefties' station.

By allowing students to choose, I preclude that my prejudices will influence how they learn. I don't want them to go one way because I told them to. I want them to make up their minds and act in their own best interests. This also prevents me from interfering with the parenting they receive at home. Moms and dads may have strong opinions on this subject and nudge their children accordingly. I don't want to interfere with that even though experience tells me it doesn't make any difference.

What do you do with your lefties?

Summer Keyboarding Class—Here are the Details

Every summer, I teach a keyboarding class to 3rd-6th graders. It's fifty minutes a day, five days a week, for three weeks. To keep myself organized and make the class as student-centered as possible for a rote sort of subject, I created a Keyboarding Wiki. There, I collected what we did each day, keyboard websites, finger exercises, teaching strategies and more. This enabled those precocious souls who didn't get enough keyboarding during the class to get more at home, though that was never required.

I start with a benchmark speed quiz to see where students were and end with one to see where they finish up. Here's what we accomplished last summer in six weeks:

- *Students increased their speed by 10%. This is better than it sounds because the first benchmark test was with uncovered keys, the final with covered*
- *Students knew the placement of all letter keys, as well as spacebar, enter, backspace, tab, escape, shift, ctrl and Alt*
- *Students developed resources to carry them through the school year when we didn't have daily practice*
- *Students enjoyed keyboarding-a major victory considering the amount of memorization required*

Here's what we do:

- Each class starts with keyboarding-Type to Learn or DanceMat Typing. I like DanceMat because it introduces keys by rows. Students also like it because of the crazy stuff the action characters do
- Each class includes finger exercises with a discussion of the importance of each finger. This addresses the common aversion to using all fingers. We do it in a circle at the front of the class-get those kids moving! To my surprise, the students love this part of the class. By Week #2, they are leading the exercises.
- Each class includes practice on a blank keyboard (see July 12th, toward the bottom for an example) to promote confidence in letter key placement, also done in a circle

at the front of class. The first week, we work on homerow, then the QWERTY row, then the lower row

- After practice with our fake keyboards, students engage in some sort of knowledge check--filling out keys on the keyboard, completing a chart of which finger went to what key, speed quiz. I have lots of options and vary them daily.
- Each class ends with keyboard practice on whichever row we are concentrating on that week. Keyboards are covered for this
- Fridays, I make different. You'll see some ideas on the wiki. After a week of keyboarding, I want them to see how it is used in environs different from straight typing (like creating a Tagxedo)
- If there is extra time, students go to any website from the Big List of Great Kids Websites.
- At the end of the three weeks, we do a Team Challenge (see Week 3, Day 5 on 'What We Did Today'). The class breaks up into groups and answers questions from a list of keyboarding issues (see the link for my list. You can create your own covering concepts you discussed). I gave each group three seconds to answer-that's it. That included conferring time. This meant they had to know the answers. This was great fun-one that I would like to do more often.

On the wiki, you'll find a few resources:

- *Keyboarding Warm-ups*
- *Keyboarding Strategies*
- *Keyboarding Websites*
- *Keyboarding Research*

For more posts from my blog on keyboarding, check these out:

1. *How Fast Should Kids Type*
2. *18 Online Keyboard Sites for Kids*
3. *Ten Best Keyboarding Hints You'll Ever See*
4. *What are Your Favorite Summer School Keyboard Activities*
5. *#55: Keyboarding in the Classroom*
6. *6 Kindergarten Keyboard Basics*
7. *How to Teach Keyboarding in Lower School*
8. *20 Best Keyboarding Websites*
9. *#57: Yes, You Should Assign Keyboarding Homework*

WHAT TO EXPECT OF YOUNGER KEYBOARDERS

Before I answer that question, let's back up a step and answer a more fundamental question: Should you expect youngers to keyboard? I'm talking about students between kindergarten and fifth grade. Are they mature enough? Do they have the fine motor skills required to use the pinkie to push the A key? Do they have that kind of focus and concentration? Should they be playing outside rather than typing at a computer?

The answer is: Yes, as a rule, though when I reviewed the literature on this subject, it is all over the place as far as when students should begin. Some say third grade; some say not until fifth or sixth. From my experience, it's third grade, though I teach pre-keyboard skills as young as kindergarten. That might be why my students are ready in third grade.

Here's a caveat: **You'll have to be the arbiter as to whether this is true for your group. If you determine your students aren't ready, wait a year.** You're the teacher. You'll know when they're ready.

Once you decide, the next question is: At what age and how fast should kids type? Here's a quick answer. Prepare kindergarteners by teaching pre-keyboard skills like posture, hand placement, mouse skills, some shortkeys. This gives their young brains and their immature fine motor skills time to develop. When you determine they're ready, move on to speed and accuracy.

Me, I've come to conclusions that fit my particular K-8 students. Their demographics include:

- private school
- parents support emphasis on keyboarding

- most have computers at home; actually, most have their own computer at home
- students are willing to practice keyboarding in class and submit homework that is oriented to keyboarding

Based on this set of students, here's what I require:

Kindergarten

An introduction. We use Type to Learn Jr. to introduce keyboarding posture and mechanics, and Brown Bear Typing to challenge them to remember key placement with no emphasis on correct fingers. My students tolerate TTL Jr. and love Brown Bear. Often, when it's free choice time, they select this program.

Here are hints to develop good habits at this young age:

- Make sure the keyboard remains in front of the student and the mouse to the right (or left for lefties). Students want to push the keyboard out of the way so they can concentrate on the mouse. Don't let them. Make it a habit to keep the keyboard centered in front of their body with the mouse comfortably on the side
- Keep hands to themselves. Don't touch others mouse, keyboard, monitor. This gives students a sense of responsibility over their own station, knowing no one can touch it but them
- Keep elbows tucked into their sides
- Keep hands curled like cat paws while typing
- Use the right thumb for the space bar
- Start students on problem solving. Yes, it takes longer to teach them how to fix their volume control, but it takes shorter in the long-run. They feel good about their skills. They remember more than you'll ever expect. They use it at home which impresses parents with your genius (OK, that's secondary, but the compliments are nice)

First Grade

More of the kindergarten introduction, with my focus on:

- sit up straight
- elbows at side

- feet in front
- hands on home row and their own side of keyboard

And, we move on to Type to Learn midway through the year. This I tell them is the 'big kids' program, one they'll use throughout Lower and Middle School. They love that.

Second Grade

I still don't discuss speed, but I begin to focus on traits that allow for speedy, accurate typing:

- good posture
- elbows at their side to force hands into the correct position
- thumb on space bar
- hands on home row
- pointers on f and j
- use the finger closest to the key while keeping pointers on f and j

This year, we don't use Type to Learn. We move into Dance Mat Typing or Nimble Fingers, where I can focus students on one keyboard row at a time. I also introduce finger exercises (which students get a kick out of) to remind them they have eight fingers and two thumbs—not just two pointers that hunt and peck.

Students work for ten minutes a week in class on only home row for a month. When they feel comfortable with key placement, I cover their hands with a cloth. They love this—see it as a badge of honor to type with hands hidden. By the end of the month, home row is memorized and they're ready for the QWERTY row. I repeat this process for the next two months with the second and third row. By the fourth month, we return to TTL4, hands covered, no matter how slowly. It feels hard at first and quickly becomes easier.

Third Grade-Fifth Grade

We start on keyboard quizzes for speed and accuracy and filling in blank keyboards for memorization. We use all the good traits acquired in K-2. As students take their speed quiz, I anecdotally notice who is using all fingers. Those that aren't lose points. Grading is based on improvement from the prior speed quiz. Students who reach the grade level standard for speed and accuracy get a free dress pass (we are a uniform school). This is exciting for them. Grade level standards are: *3rd Grade: 15 wpm, 4th Grade: 25 wpm, 5th Grade: 30 wpm*

I add five hints to the kindergarten list that appeal to the more mature mind:

- Use inside fingers for inside keys, outside fingers for outside keys
- Use the finger closest to the key you need. Sounds simple, but this isn't what usually happens with beginners.
- Play your keyboard like you do a piano (or violin, or guitar, or recorder). You'd never use your pointer for all keys
- Fingers move, not your hands. Hands stay anchored to the f and j keys
- Don't use caps lock for capitals! Use shift.

What do you use for Lower School keyboarding? I'd love to hear from you.

THE ELEPHANTINE IMPACT OF TECHNOLOGY ON EDUCATION

Have you noticed what's happening in your child's school? Technology. There's rarely a lesson taught, be it math or science or health, that doesn't include some form of technology to enhance its message, increase its reach, improve its communication. If you haven't been in the classroom lately, drop by this week when you pick up your wonderful student. There's likely to be a Smartboard (or some sort of interactive screen) on the wall, a pod of computers (if not 1:1 laptops) overflowing from a corner, maybe iPads on desktops or in a mobile cart, a digital camera and microphones to record events, streaming video from Discovery Channel. Those ubiquitous samples of student work that traditionally clutter the walls now include many created with computers.

Today's education happens by standing on the shoulders of technology innovation.

If you don't have a school-age child, take a peek at Cisco's VNI Service Adoption blog. There's an uptick in the impact of technology on all parts of consumer life. As Cisco suggests, these changes are all about connecting students to their future, empowering them with responsibility for their own education in areas such as:

- access to learning
- quality of instruction and education assessment
- innovative learning models
- decision making
- reduced costs with administrative efficiency (not yet, but it's a good goal)

As a tech teacher, the new educational paradigm relies on either the United States' No Child Left Behind, the International

Baccalaureate Organization's international IB educational guidelines, and/or the National Board of Governors state-driven Common Core Standards (already adopted in 46 states). Interestingly, these education standards may (or may not) address technology, but only tangentially, as they contribute to core subjects. Many states have area-specific technology standards (though all don't, most visibly California). Others leave it to the International Society of Technology Education's well-respected NETS national technology standards.

As the tech teacher, I used to teach keyboarding and software. Now, depending upon my school's focus, it's laptops, iPads, online tools, websites, and problem-solving to increase independence.

Over the next months, I'll give you a peek into how today's classrooms are using this unprecedented access to the world's knowledge base. I'll start with keyboarding.

It's not your mother's typing class. First off, it starts in kindergarten. I bet most of you took typing in high school—middle school if your school district was precocious.

What a wonderful time to be a student.

HOW TO TEACH INTERNET SAFETY IN K-6

The Internet is a wonderful resource for kids for researching school reports, communicating with teachers, staying in touch with friends, and entertaining themselves. They can literally hit a few keystrokes and find out about culture in China, the history of Europe, or take a tour of the American White House.

But with access comes risks, even if you're careful. For example, in our class project on life cycles, we never allow the students to search "chicks", rather they must type "baby chickens" to avoid the problems the former carries.

The digital natives we are educating don't want to hide from these sorts of problems, though. They want to learn to manage them. What we as teachers must do is show them how to avoid the internet's bad neighborhoods so they can benefit from the good. Here's my year-by-year teaching run-down:

Kindergarten

I mix internet safety lessons in with other teaching during my 45-minutes-per-week lesson. I spread it out throughout the year, repeating if necessary, which doesn't bother kindergartners.

- First time students access the internet, I provide an overview. What is it? Where does it go? What will they see once they've clicked a link? How should they safely use a link? How do they NOT click on the ads (and what are 'ads')?
- We visit age-appropriate videos that teach online safety
    - Surf Swell Island
    - Clicky's Quest-internet safety

- Clicky's Web World-What to do
- Princess who knew how to UYN-video
- Webonauts
- Garfield-internet safety
- Webville Outlaws-internet safety
- My Online Neighborhood-video
- Internet safety video-a day in a digital citizen's life
- Safe surfing ebook—read or read to you
- Internet Safety Site -Disney

- Have sufficient adult assistance that student activities can be corrected immediately so learning is seamless and students aren't confused

First Grade

I mix these lessons in with other teaching throughout the year. I reinforce the topic at least monthly so students realize its importance.

- Remind students of the lessons learned about the internet safety in kindergarten-what is it? Where does it go? What will they see once they've clicked a link? How should they safely use a link? How do they NOT click on the ads (and what are 'ads')?
    - Bad Guy Patrol
    - Computer safety-videos
    - Surf Swell Island
    - Clicky's Quest-internet safety
    - Clicky's Web World-What to do
    - Princess who knew how to UYN-video
    - Webonauts
    - Internet safety video-a day in a digital citizen's life
    - Garfield-internet safety
    - Webville Outlaws-internet safety
    - My Online Neighborhood-video
    - Safe surfing ebook—read or read to you

Second Grade

- For 15-30 minutes of one weekly lesson: Discuss ***image copyright*** as your students search for online pictures in conjunction with a class report—what that is, why it's important, how to identify a copyrighted image. Here are several websites with copyright-free images:
    - Creative Commons
    - Flikr-they list their restrictions-this is a good learning tool
    - Flikrcc-only creative commons images on Flikr
    - Free Photo
    - Morgue File-free images, but check the licenses first
    - Open Clip Art
    - Open Photo
    - Smithsonian Wild-200,000 animal pictures!
    - Stock Exchange
    - Wiki Images
- For one lesson during the year: Discuss ***online presenc**e* as you create an online story in Storybird or Blabberize.
- Reinforce **cybersafety and online security** by creating an avatar using one of these free web-based avatar creators:
    - Lego
    - Build your Wild Self
    - Voki
- Research a project that goes to specific websites as a method of teaching ***safe search methods***
- During sponge or free time before/after a project: Visit these online websites:
    - Internet safety online
    - Internet Smart Princess
    - Surf Swell Island
    - Internet safety video-a day in a digital citizen's life
    - Faux Paws Internet Safety
    - Garfield internet safety
    - Internet safety
    - Who are your online friends?

Third Grade—this is a four-week unit

- Create avatars as you discuss **internet safety.** Use:
    - Lego

- Build your Wild Self
- Voki

- Discuss **online netiquette**
- Discuss **copyrights**
- Discuss **plagiarism**
- Websites to visit throughout the semester, during free time before/after projects:
    - Safety Land—with certificate at end
    - Safe Kids Quiz

Fourth Grade—this is a five-week unit

- Create avatars as you discuss **internet safety**
- Discuss **safe research** methods (and how that equates to internet safety)
- Discuss **netiquette**, good online manners
- Discuss **copyrights**
- Discuss **plagiarism**
- Websites we visit (given time)

    - Plagiarism video
    - Privacy Playground—age 8-10
    - Safe Kids Quiz
    - Internet Safety
    - CyberSense and Nonsense

Fifth Grade—this is a seven-week unit

- Discuss **digital citizenship**—what that means, why it's important, the responsibilities of being a 'digital citizen'
- Discuss **copyrights**
- Discuss **plagiarism** and the importance of giving credit to the creator of text and images
- Discuss **fair use**
- Discuss **public domain**
- Discuss **'digital footprint'**—what's that mean?
- Discuss **netiquette**, good online manners
- Discuss **safe online presence** (no last names, etc.)
- Discuss **safe research** methods (and how that equates to internet safety)
- Webquest on Hoax or Not

- Website on Is This Picture Real?

Sixth Grade (and Teens)

- Self-directed online internet safety unit

Here are tips suggested by many Police Departments as good general rules for kids accessing the internet:

- *Tell your parents immediately if you come across something that makes you feel uncomfortable. Remember that people on the Internet may not be who they seem.*
- *Never give out identifying information such as your name, home address, school name or telephone number in a public message, such as in a chat room or on a bulletin board.*
- *People who are dangerous may represent themselves online as a young boy or girl to entice you to a face-to-face meeting.*
- *You should never arrange a face-to-face meeting without first asking a parent. If a parent agrees, you should meet in a public place with your parent accompanying you. Be careful when someone offers you something for nothing.*
- *Be very careful about any offers that involve you coming to a meeting or have someone visit your home.*
- *Always get to know your online friends just as you would get to know all of your friends.*
- *Never send your picture without first asking a parent.*
- *Never respond to messages or items that are suggestive, obscene, belligerent, threatening or make you feel uncomfortable.*
- *Be sure that you are dealing with someone you and your parents know and trust before giving out any personal information about yourself.*
- *Diligent parental supervision will help ensure your safety on the Internet.*

IS KEYBOARDING DEAD?

I was on one of my tech teacher forums—where I keep up to date on changes in education and technology—and stumbled into a heated discussion about what grade level is best to begin the focus on typing (is fifth grade too old—or too young?). Several teachers shared that keyboarding was the cornerstone of their elementary-age technology program. Others confessed their Admin wanted it eliminated as unnecessary. Still others dismissed the discussion as moot: Tools like Dragon Speak (the standard in speech recognition software) and iPhone's wildly-popular Siri mean keyboarding will soon be as useful as cursive and floppy discs.

My knee jerk reaction was 'That's years off', but it got me thinking. Is it really? Or are the fires of change about to sweep through our schools? Already, families are succumbing to the overwhelming popularity of touch screens in the guise of iPads. No typing required—just a finger poke, a sweep, and the command is executed. Those clumsy, losable styluses of your parent's era are so last generation. The day kids discover how easy it is to tell their phones what they need done (think iPhone 4S)—stick a fork in it; keyboarding will be done.

Truthfully, as someone who carefully watches ed tech trends, a discussion about the importance of keyboarding says as much about national education expectations as typing. Schools are moving away from reports and essays as methods of assessing understanding. Teachers want plays that act out a topic, student-created videos that demonstrate authentic understanding, multi-media magazines that convey a deeper message. Web-based communication tools like Voki, Animoto, and Glogster—all of which have limited typing—are de rigueur in every academic program that purports to be tech-savvy. Students are encouraged to use audio, visual, taped vignettes, recorded snippets—everything that ISN'T the traditional MS Word document with a bullet list of comprehensive points to convey the message. For much of what students want out of life—to call a friend, find their location on GPS, arrange a get-together, create a reminder—writing is passé. Email to your middle school and high school children is as anachronistic as snail mail. Even texting is being shunted aside by vlogs and Skype, and note-taking—with the popularity of apps like Evernote—has become something best accomplished with swipes and clicks.

That's what's killing keyboarding.

But it's not dead yet. Certainly, voice commands can activate a software program or bring up the teacher's website to view homework, but how do you quietly talk to a computer during a lecture? Are programs like Dragon Speak and Siri capable of blocking out extraneous sounds and focusing in on the singular human voice? And don't discount the aesthetics of typing. Take me for example. I'm a K-8 technology teacher. I'm in the know about the latest and greatest in technology trends. I'm expected to try them—and use them. I write for a hobby, but I have arthritis. My doctor wants me to stop typing, switch to Dragon Speak. My modern kids are all for it, but Dragon Speak's quirkiness (like mis-typing oh-so-many words) is distracting. Plus, there's a connection between my brain and fingers that helps me think. Maybe it's as simple as I muse at the speed I type. Maybe the clackity-clack of the keys is soothing to my rattled brain. Nothing in my pedagogic or anecdotal research has convinced me it isn't also true for kids. If we eliminate the peaceful predictability of tapping fingers on those little squares, will getting words on paper be more difficult?

I wonder.

What do you think?

More Technology Books for your Classroom

Name

Address

Email

Phone Number

Which book?	**Price (print/ebook/ Combo)**	**How Many?**	**P&H ($4.50/bk) ($2.99/ebk)**	**Total**
Kindergarten Tech Textbook	*$18.99/$14.99/$30.99*			
1st Grade Tech Textbook	*$22.99/$14.99/$32.99*			
2nd Grade Tech Textbook	*$22.99/$14.99/$32.99*			
3rd Grade Tech Textbook	*$22.99/$14.99/$32.99*			
4th Grade Tech Textbook	*$22.99/$16.99/$34.99*			
5th Grade Tech Textbook	*$22.99/$17.99/$36.99*			
6th Grade Tech Textbook	*$25.99/18.99/$38.99*			
K-6 Combo (all 7 textbooks)	*$143.97/$99.97/$219.99*			
55 Tech Projects—Volume I	*$32.99/$16.99/$47.99*			
55 Tech Projects—Volume II	*$32.99/$16.99/$47.99*			
Toolkit Combo—VI and II	*$59.99/$36.99/$85.97*			
35 More Projects for K-6	*$20.97 (digital only)*			
30 Common Core SS Projects	*$20.97 (digital only)*			
98 Tech Tips From Classroom	*$9.99 (digital only)*			
16 Holiday Projects	*$6.99 (digital only)*			
19 Posters for the Tech Lab	*$6.99 (digital only)*			
38 Web 2.0 Articles	*$2.99 (digital only)*			
	Total			

Fill out this form (prices subject to change).
Email Zeke.rowe@structuredlearning.net.
Pay via Paypal, Amazon, Google Ebooks or pre-approved school district PO.
Questions? Contact Zeke Rowe.

Structured Learning
http://structuredlearning.net
AskaTechTeacher.com
Zeke Rowe